THRIVING
LIFE

THRIVING
LIFE

HOW TO LIVE YOUR BEST LIFE
NO MATTER THE CARDS YOU'RE DEALT

Professor
LAURA BERG

Health Communications, Inc.
Boca Raton, Florida

www.hcibooks.com

**Library of Congress Cataloging-in-Publication Data
is available through the Library of Congress**

© 2021 Laura Berg

ISBN-13: 978-0-7573-2396-6 (Paperback)
ISBN-10: 0-7573-2396-0 (Paperback)
ISBN-13: 978-0-7573-2397-3 (ePub)
ISBN-10: 0-7573-2397-9 (ePub)

Publisher: Health Communications, Inc.
      1700 NW 2nd Avenue
      Boca Raton, FL 33432-1653

Cover design by Larissa Hise Henoch
Interior design by Larissa Hise Henoch, formatting by Lawna Patterson Oldfield
Author photo by Anna Epp

CONTENTS

ACKNOWLEDGMENTS

To my husband, Moe, thank you for always providing me comfort and safety. For understanding and supporting who I am completely and without judgment. Thank you for being my security, the person I can always depend on and trust. You are my rock, my love, and my best friend.

To my daughter, Fireese, I admire your passion and strength more than you'll ever know. You are self-aware and resilient and always strive to seek betterment and growth, even when it is difficult. I am in awe of who you are. You are fearless in your ability to tackle challenges, and I can't wait to see all that you will achieve in the future.

To my son, Hartford, you are the kindest, most caring and compassionate soul I know. You teach me how to be a better person through your empathy for others. My wish for you is that you never lose your kind and open heart. You are destined to touch people's lives in a meaningful way.

To my friend, Holly, *Thriving Life* would not exist had it not been for you telling me I should write a book. You never made me feel damaged, but the opposite; you made me feel strong and resilient. Thank you for always being a supportive ear.

To Louisa, thank you for always reminding me that my mom would be proud of me. I'm grateful that you came into our lives and became a surrogate grandmother to my children and a loving friend to me. I am always and forever grateful for your love and support.

To my brother, Jason, I hope you are at peace.

To my birth parents, thank you for giving me life.

And finally, this book is dedicated to my mom, Lenna. You are not alive to see the finished product, but I know you would be proud. You are and have always been my inspiration to be a better person. No matter what life threw at you, you would put a smile on your face and handle all adversities with grace. You are my hero.

INTRODUCTION

New beginnings are often disguised
as painful endings.

—Lao Tzu

I t took me forty-five years to realize that most people have some sort of shadow following them. I grew up with so many shadows, feeling sorry for myself all the time. We were poor. The years were filled with abuse. My home never felt secure.

As a child of adoption, I always felt that I could have had a different life, a better life. I was envious of everyone I met. How could I be so unlucky? It wasn't until very recently that I realized all those people I envied had carried their own shames and traumas. People hid unpleasant things like poverty, abuse, mental illness, and emotional neglect.

I'm not sure how we became so closed as a society. Imagine how great the world would be if sharing, openness, and support were the norm. Instead, we find ourselves in a world where people share happy photos online that paint a false reality. People are programmed to share happiness and the positives in their lives and shy away from sharing hardships and struggles. I am guilty of doing this too. When we ask someone, "How are you?" the expected answer is, "good" or "fine." If we didn't paint this fake sense of well-being in our public personas, maybe we would all feel more "normal" with our true realities. I often wonder how my mental health would be today if I knew that I wasn't alone in my suffering. I am incredibly grateful for my life today, but it was a struggle to get here—a long, hard, painful struggle.

I've made it this far and now I want to share my life experiences—how I not only survived them but also found a way to be better in spite of them. Or more appropriately, I'm better because of them. Who knows? My experience has taught me I'm not alone in the horrible circumstances that life has thrown at me. We've all had bad things happen to us. Finding hardships isn't difficult; the challenge is overcoming those hardships.

I always thought some people were lucky enough that they lived a life free of bad experiences. And maybe some people are lucky, but those people are four-leaf clovers in a vast field of regular clovers. The people who seem to be living a charmed life are just people who decided life wasn't going to knock them down. They put in the work every day to feel better and overcome life's adversities. Elsewhere, people who seem to have it all often don't. If they did, then larger-than-life people like Marilyn Monroe and Robin Williams wouldn't have died by suicide.

I remember when Robin Williams died. It shook the world because he was one of those lucky, seemingly untouchable people with money, fame, friends, family, and laughter. He seemed to embody happiness. But Robin Williams fought his own battle with depression and lost. We tend to look at other people and think their lives are easy because they have money, a stable job, a car, two parents at home, or any number of happiness indicators. We see what is lacking in our lives through the lives of others, and we envy that. Meanwhile, they envy someone else for a totally different reason.

If you are unhappy and want your life to change, then you have to put the work in. Change doesn't come because you want it. Change occurs because you make it happen.

Say there is a person named Pat who is a receptionist and unhappy in her job and life. Her unhappiness is largely because she is sitting behind a desk all day, answering phones and filing papers. She continually wishes she could be somewhere else, do something else, and be more fulfilled. One day Pat decides she wants to be a marine biologist. She loves the ocean, loves sea life, and wants desperately to work outside and throw her office job away. So Pat sits down, updates her résumé, and starts searching for her dream career. Every time she finds a posting for anything resembling a marine biologist job, she emails her résumé with an inspiring cover letter showing her passion for wanting to work in the ocean. She waits.

Two years go by, and Pat is still mailing out her résumé. She's now angry and defeated and still in the job that makes her unhappy. Pat wanted to be a marine biologist, but she had no education or work experience in that field. How on earth did she think she was going to get a job simply because she wanted it? She spent two years doing tasks that would never lead to what she wanted. Pat should have used those two years to go back to school and properly train herself. When a friend asked her why she didn't do that, she said because she thought that would be too hard.

Though she wanted her life to be different, Pat wasn't ready to take the steps necessary in order to make that change. Learn from Pat.

By picking up this book, you've taken the first step to bettering yourself. You want something to change in your life. Whatever it is, now is the time to commit and put in the work to reach the happiness that you want and deserve. Don't be Pat. Don't just pick up a book and read it and hope things will change. Pick up this book, read it, and act on the advice within. Make an effort to implement the things that inspire you. Keep this book close by and return to it whenever you need it. You are the navigator of your life. Don't sit in the back seat and hope things will change. Get behind the wheel and drive!

Throughout this book, I am going to share some of the significant lows I've experienced in my life and how I overcame them. The most important takeaway is that you must start by loving yourself. This is one of the hardest things for people to do. You can hate your circumstances, your job, where you live, how your family treats you, and so on. But you must stop hating yourself. If you don't love yourself, how can you expect others to love you?

This is mental work that you are going to have to put in every day until you finally believe in yourself and feel that you are worthy of love. That means reminding yourself to love and accept who you are. You can't start to work on any form of life change until you love who you are and want to protect and value that person.

It has taken me forty-five years to reach the point where I love myself and I am confident in who I've become. I have a job I love and a wonderful family, and I am surrounded by trusted friends. Throughout those forty-five years, I worked hard. I had many more downs than ups. I felt sorry for myself more times than I can count. I've suffered from severe depression since I was sixteen. I still suffer from depression, but I've found coping mechanisms to keep at my disposal for when I need them. Part of that is knowing the signs that I'm slipping into depression and taking action to correct my course. It took me years to learn how to recognize those signs and do something before I fell into the big black vortex that depression can be.

I am a professor and trained therapist with specialties in cognitive behavioral therapy (CBT) and dialectical behavior therapy (DBT), but I have also lived everything I'm sharing in this book. I've lived through abuse. I've experienced numerous forms of rejection; one was so severe that it shaped how I viewed myself and how I believed others viewed me. I've hurt myself and wanted to die more than once. I have tried to end my life and, thankfully, didn't succeed. I've lived with depression for almost thirty years. And, I've survived a life that could have sent me down a very different and unhealthy path.

I am not under any delusion that life will be a bed of roses now that I've learned all these coping techniques. But I do know that I will get past any garbage that is thrown my way. I will continue to put the work into bettering my life. I will continue to love myself even though that's not always easy.

During my educational and life journey, I learned that no one tool is the solution to all problems. I want you to think about your journey to happiness as akin to building a house. Would you build a house with just a hammer? No, of course not. While a hammer would be essential, you also need saws, screwdrivers, drills, wrenches, and a litany of other tools to help you build a sturdy and supportive house.

I believe that you can do this, that you can pull yourself out of whatever hole you're in and come out the other side stronger. I want to teach you how. With this book, I want you to feel like you are a part of something bigger and see that you are not alone. Together, we can overcome. Together, we are strong.

CHAPTER ONE

Stop Being a Victim

I am not what happened to me,
I am what I choose to become.

—Carl Gustav Jung

E ach of us walks around with a bunch of different "people" inside playing different roles at different times in our lives. These selves are the central building blocks of the psyche. One of the most powerful, loud "people" is *victim*.

I was a victim most of my life. My childhood was never easy; I faced several terrible traumas throughout my early years. Growing up, and for a big part of my adult life, I was unable to move past certain events, and I continued to let those experiences define me.

I grew up very poor and felt poor every day of my life. I never had the toys that my friends had. I never had the new clothes or the expensive shoes. I never invited people over to my house because I didn't want them to know how poor I was. Constantly jealous of people because it seemed like everyone had more than me, I walked around for years with my victim self, shouting, "Poor me!"

I remember the Care Bears plush fad. Seemingly everyone had them, and we were defined by the type of bear we had. They were beautiful with amazingly soft fur, cute faces, and the best chest decals with the various Care Bear powers. I wanted one so badly. Every single girl in my school had one (or so it seemed). My mom knew I was upset, so she went to the craft store and bought what she needed to make me a Care Bear. She spent hours sewing it so I could fit in with all the other girls.

But instead of appreciating her selfless gesture, I was horrified. The bear was ugly and fake, and everyone would make fun of me. I was a victim of being poor once again by having the knockoff instead of the expensive real thing. Of course, I was a little kid and didn't know better, but looking back now, I wish I could have appreciated what I had. I should have appreciated the hours of love my mom put into making that bear for me. I wasn't a victim. I was loved.

I carried that feeling of being a victim into my adult life. I am grateful now that I no longer view my childhood that way. I am no longer a victim. I am strong because I learned how to accept that you can't have everything, and how to deal with adversity and survive it.

The Care Bears example is just a small, benign example of how my perception of events stayed with me and shaped how I felt about myself and my life. Throughout this chapter and book, I will touch upon more malignant traumatic experiences I faced and how I overcame those negative events to become healthier and happier. This is just one example of how changing the way you view things can change the way you feel about yourself, and how our actions and reactions can define us.

Getting in Touch with the Inner Victim

The positive purpose of the victim is to become focused on self. It allows us to be vulnerable and ask for help. But this can only happen once the victim realizes that they need to stop being a victim and make positive changes.

Cognitive behavioral therapy (CBT) is great for the victim mentality because it can help turn the victim into a survivor. CBT helps us change the way we think about past events and the control they have over us. Don't allow past events or people to continue to victimize you today. Take control of your life, the people you have in it, and the way you view yourself. You are strong because you are alive and have survived your past traumas. Sometimes it may feel like you are barely surviving and that you aren't living the life you wish you could be. I get it. It takes hard work to overcome your past traumas and to not only live, but thrive. By reading this book you are taking a step in the right direction. Start by telling yourself, "I am no longer a victim; I am a survivor."

Self-Sabotage and the Victim

Self-sabotage goes hand-in-hand with the victim mentality —you often can't have one without the other. The victim makes you believe that the circumstances are out of your control, that someone will come to your aid, or that the world owes you something. The victim use statements like, "The world owes me because…." This is an extremely destructive belief. When you listen to the victim's voice inside your mind, you stop looking for solutions.

It's important to be brutally honest with yourself and take notice if you have been claiming to be a victim. Is that where you want to stay? Coming out of the victim mentality takes courage, brutal honesty with yourself, and a desire to be a responsible, happy adult.

Part of being a responsible adult is taking responsibility for your life, where it is today, and where you are headed. It doesn't matter how far in the hole you are; there is a way to get out and then get to where you want to be. Step one in this journey is honesty. Without that, your best-laid plans will be futile and will not give you the results you want. It's like planning a trip to California but putting your starting point as Texas when you are actually in Chicago.

For a big chunk of my life, I wasn't being honest with myself. I was lying by not addressing the horrible events of my past. Growing up, I experienced physical and mental abuse from my father and sexual abuse from my grandfather. The past traumas I suffered were driving my relationships and the way I viewed my worth. I didn't want to think about my past and how it was negatively affecting my present. I wanted to ignore it and pretend it didn't happen. By ignoring the significant role my past traumas were playing, I was creating issues for myself that I didn't even realize I was doing.

During my CBT training, I realized what I was doing in my adult life was continuing to allow my father and grandfather to victimize me. They were no longer in my life. They had no power over me. But, by continuing to dwell on what happened, I was giving them control. And it made me angry. One day I decided to refuse giving them any more control over my life.

I changed the way I thought about past events. The little girl who suffered the abuse was a victim. I am sad for her and what she went through, but I am no longer that little girl. I can't let that little girl continue to make the adult me feel like a victim. I am not a victim; I am a survivor. There is power in words, and simply changing the way you talk about something can be liberating. I have no shame in admitting that I am an amazing person who has overcome so much and came out stronger on the other side. I refuse to give anyone the power to make me feel less of a person or to make me feel like a victim. I am in control of who I am and the life I live.

Be Honest With Yourself

Be honest with yourself to discover why you play the victim. Is it because you want sympathy or attention? Do you lack the self-confidence to express your own needs and wants? Do you bully and attempt to control those around you? Do you see life as a constant threat? Do you view others as being out to cause you harm? These are all belief systems that need to be looked at in a safe environment and, indeed, many victims need the help of a therapist to understand their behavior and how to move beyond it.

Looking back at your family is often a good place to start when asking how you became a victim. How was the relationship with your parents and other family members? Was there any physical or mental abuse? Did you feel secure at home? Did you feel loved? This needs to be done without judgment. It is a fact-finding mission to evaluate and understand your perspective on victimhood.

For most, the result of this work will be an understanding that you are lacking self-worth and confidence. You may feel you are not important or worthy and cannot relate to others in any other way.

Once you have begun this journey of self-honesty, you will begin to be able to take responsibility for your own actions and behavior. You will no longer blame your behavior on someone in your past or someone else in your life today. You can talk about the good things that have happened and let go of the list of problems that you usually start conversations with. Let go of the negative self-talk and embrace healthy boundary setting and interactions. Try to see the good in everyone, including yourself.

Once you begin to change your behavior, you will find that self-respect follows. You will become more attuned to how you show respect for others and learn to receive attention for positive behaviors and actions.

Letting go of the past is not always easy, especially if you have been a victim for a long time. But the smallest changes that you make will have positive ramifications in your life and provide the opportunity for continued growth. Eliminating the victim mentality from your life will allow you to understand that you deserve to be loved and cared for.

Stop Thinking Like a Victim

Casting yourself in the role of victim destroys your self-esteem and can cause mental health issues. This victim mentality can sabotage your ability to live a fruitful and rewarding life because you believe you are not worthy. Allowing your inner victim to control your thought process can weaken your confidence, restrict your options, and block your ability to reach for your dreams because you convince yourself that you do not deserve happiness.

Believing you are a victim and acting like one can have seriously negative effects on your relationships. Think for a moment about people who immerse themselves in the victim role. They are not much fun to be around. If you tend to dwell on the "poor me" mentality, consciously or subconsciously, then people will tend to avoid being around you. This can lead to loneliness and feeling once again like you are a victim, so the cycle of victimhood continues. Addressing your victimhood and changing the way you think about your past can have positive impacts on your present.

Martin Seligman, the world-renowned positive psychologist, explains that "victimology"—placing blame on other people or circumstances for our problems—is directly related to the concept of learned helplessness. Learned helplessness is a phenomenon where an individual believes that his or her actions make no difference in how things turn out. The victim role is a form of self-pity.

It is not only your right, but more importantly, your responsibility to decide if the victim role serves you or imprisons you. In my experience, the victim mentality is a form of psychological paralysis. No matter who or what has "done you wrong," it will not bring you psychological health or self-confidence to embrace the victim mentality.

Recovering from Being a Victim

Victims are often people that have grown up in households where the mother or father demonstrated the role of victim to them. If one parent was abusive toward the other, the child may identify with the abused individual. As they get older, they will accept being bullied or abused in their own relationships because that is what they have witnessed growing up. On the other hand, children and adults who have not seen abuse tend to have the ability to stand up for themselves and leave unhealthy situations to seek more appropriate interactions relatively quickly.

Victims make up one half of the picture. When there is a victim, there is almost always a perpetrator. In some situations, the person playing the victim in one situation may be the perpetrator in another, which could be a reaction to the abuse. Very often, children who are bullies at school are experiencing abuse at home, either by a sibling or a parent figure.

There are other events that create victims besides growing up in a family of abusers and victims. Sometimes, a victim is born as a result of a traumatic event, where the safety of the person is threatened to such a degree that they become very fearful of the world and life. Their reaction to the event is one where they become convinced that the world is negative and that misfortune seeks them out.

No one ever sets out to be a victim, and no one would ever choose the role. The behaviors are either learned or imposed. Either way, many people play this role unconsciously and get their attention from their misfortune, illness, or pain.

Seeking recovery from victimhood can only happen once the problem has been recognized for what it is. This can be a gradual process of understanding how unsatisfying your current behavior is. Often, the desire for change develops over time when relationships falter, friends disappear, and being miserable becomes too painful.

My brother was unable to get past his victimhood. We were both adopted, coming from two different sets of parents. We were nothing alike. He had black hair; mine was blonde. He had brown eyes; mine were blue. He was loud and outspoken; I was quiet and shy. We may not have shared the same blood, but that didn't matter to him. I was his little sister, and he loved me with all his being.

Sometimes it felt like our lives came out of the book series *A Series of Unfortunate Events*. Misfortune and trauma consumed our lives year after year but, through it all, as long as I had my brother, I knew I'd be fine. When we were kids, my brother took the brunt of the abuse. If I got in trouble, my brother would try to protect me by saying he had made the mistake. He would get the strap instead of me. He was my protector.

When my parents divorced, my brother was in a juvenile detention center. His response to the abuse was turning to drugs and alcohol and a life of crime at a young age. It was his escape. When he got out of the detention center, he went back to live with my father, his abuser. He'd turn again to alcohol, drugs, and crime and end up in jail. He'd get out of jail, live with my father, and the cycle would continue.

One day I was talking to my brother, and he confided in me that his friend just died from an intentional overdose. I asked him what an *intentional* overdose was, and he said, "When you are on methadone, you don't take heroin unless you want to kill yourself. Every heroin addict knows this." The last time my brother got out of jail, he was scared to go live with my father but felt he had no other place to go. A few days later, I got the news that my brother had died of an overdose.

My whole extended family was sad for his wasted life but not sad for him. In their eyes, he was just a druggie who overdosed. However, I knew the truth. My brother was on methadone when he left prison. He went out and scored heroin with the intent of ending his life. He could no longer go on with the awful cycle of victimhood.

If only he had been honest with himself about staying in the cycle of abuse and continuing to let our father victimize him. There were options for him. He just didn't know how to exercise those options because he was so consumed with being a victim. I wish I knew then what I know now and could have helped him become the amazing person I know he would have been.

The first step to escaping the grasp of victimhood sounds simple, but it is much harder than you might think, and it's the most essential step.

The "Way Out" of Victimhood

The second step, after being honest with yourself, is finding a way out of victimhood. It is simple: accountability and self-responsibility. These are the tools that release you from the quicksand of victimization. When you become account-able and self-responsible, you give yourself ownership of your actions and the ability to achieve the (realistic) results you set for yourself.

I want you to take a pencil and paper and answer the fol-lowing questions. You don't have to answer them all at once. Sit with the questions and really give yourself time to think of your responses.

1. Are there areas of your life where you consider yourself a victim?

2. Do you ever consider how you may be contributing to your feelings of being victimized? How do you feel when you even consider this question?

3. Has anyone ever suggested you were acting like a victim? What was it like to hear that?

4. Did you ever feel like a victim when you were growing up? Did your parents or primary caregivers ever make you feel like you were not "good enough"?

5. Did your parents or primary caregivers ever overtly or covertly indi-cate they felt like victims?

6. Do you have a spiritual life, that is, meditation, self-reflection, journaling, walking quietly in nature?

7. What do you think the "blueprint" for your life is, meaning your life purpose or why you're here?

If you've had something horrible happen to you, I am so sorry. But if you allow that thing to continue to have power over you, then you are continuing to allow that person or situation to keep victimizing you. Don't give it that control.

The term *self-fulfilling prophecy* means that if you are told something enough times, you begin to believe it. This has been proven time and time again. If someone tells a child he or she is dumb over and over again, then that child begins to believe they are dumb. The opposite is also true. If you tell a child he or she is smart and capable, then the child believes that, which helps him or her become smart and capable. Words are powerful and can make us believe one thing or another.

I remember watching an episode of *Brain Games*, during which they had people try to shoot basketballs into a net. Every time they missed, a crowd of people booed. The contestants became flustered and missed most of the ten shots they took. Then they repeated the experiment by being blindfolded. Each time they took a shot, the crowd cheered. They didn't get the basketball in most times, but they *believed* they did because the crowd cheered for them. Finally, they took the blindfolds off and tried shooting again. In every case, the person scored more baskets in that final round. This is because their brains told them they could make the shot, they *believed* they could, and so they did.

The brain is a powerful thing. The beliefs you have and the words you tell yourself can change the way your life unfolds. Overcoming this victim mentality is central to improving self-esteem and can oftentimes be a start on your road to recovery. It may require joining groups, reading books, and meditating every day. Over the course of this journey, you will begin to see yourself as perfectly acceptable just the way you are. You will be confident that you are okay and have found a new way to live.

It took me a long time to come to this realization of self-honesty, of my own victimhood, of how I could pull myself out of this mind-set and move forward. I was so tired of allowing my past to define me and my future. When I was finally honest with myself, everything changed. It is possible for you to face your past—your anxieties and traumas—and come out the other side of this journey a strong, confident person ready to fulfill your purpose in the world.

CHAPTER TWO

Talk Minus Action Gives You Nothing

Do nothing, and nothing happens.

—Mhairi McFarlane

I love the quote above. It really makes me stop and think about how we should live our lives. One day, while trying to figure out what I wanted to do with my life, my husband shared that quote with me. It made total sense. Of course, if I sat back and hoped something would happen for me without doing anything to make it happen, then it wouldn't happen.

Many of us are afraid to take chances because we might fail, but if we don't take chances or simply do nothing, then failure is guaranteed. We need to take control of the events in our lives and be prepared to deal with the bad that comes with the good. That means being able to handle failure and rejection, and not letting the setbacks stop us from moving forward and trying new things.

Welcoming failure as part of life is not easy, but with a little work, you can learn to accept failure with grace and move forward.

The first step is knowing that there are many paths to achieving your goal to a happy life. Even though we make plans, life is unpredictable. If one plan fails, it is essential to our success that we find a new path to our goals and happiness.

When I was twenty-four, I worked in an office and hated it. I dreaded getting up every morning to face a job where I felt unfulfilled. My boyfriend at the time, now husband, asked me, "If you could do anything, what would you do?"

I'd always wanted to be a teacher, but at that time it was next to impossible to get into a teachers college. He suggested that I research all my options and then shared the quote that I remind myself of often: "If you do nothing, nothing happens." I'd never become a teacher if I never did anything to make it happen.

So, I sat down and filled out what felt like a hundred applications. Within a few months, I received endless rejection letters. Every single application I sent came back as a "no." I was devastated and ready to give up. I felt that I was destined to be in a dead-end job that I hated.

There was one other option left, but it felt incredibly unrealistic—attending college in another country. That would mean paying international student fees, which were ridiculously high. Even though the college was just a short drive across the border, that weekly commute and overnight stay would make the cost of going to that school very expensive—the type of money I didn't have.

I decided not to let money deter me right away. I attended

an information session at one of the colleges and discovered there were a number of different solutions that made my dream slightly more attainable. It became clear to me this was my path to becoming a teacher. I applied to a program at Daemen College and was accepted.

For a year, I was a full-time nanny working ten-hour days, Monday through Thursday and half a day on Friday. At noon on Fridays, I'd hop in my car and drive the two to three hours to Buffalo for my 3:30 PM class. I'd be in school Friday night and all day Saturday, and then I'd drive back home only to start a waitressing shift that ended at 3:00 AM early Sunday morning.

Sunday was my only day off. It was an exhausting schedule, but I knew it was a means to an end. I wanted to become a teacher, and I was going to do whatever I could to make that happen.

You must take action to be successful in life and especially in your career. What kind of action should you take and when? Start with a clear vision of what you want to achieve and affirm it in your thoughts as a belief—believe that you can have it. This sets off a process which inevitably brings your intention into the physical world. My vision was to become a teacher. I *believed* I could become a teacher and I explored every path. I achieved my goal of becoming a teacher because I made it happen.

How to Attain Goals

If you aim at nothing, you will go through life never hitting anything. Life will be a slow crawl to nowhere. It is very easy to become trapped in the mode of setting goals, failing to achieve them, and consequently giving up on goals and dreams. But this does not have to be you.

Start with visualizing your dreams and goals. Never allow others to tell you that you can't do something. Believe in yourself and believe that you hold the power to control the choices you make to reach those goals. You will be amazed at how easy it is to hit the target when you believe you can. No matter what it is you would like to achieve, you will only hit what you aim for.

When I graduated teachers college, it was the year the local government decided to cut spending for education. Because of this, there would be no teaching jobs for new teachers. My classmates were stressing about getting on the substitute-teaching list for their local board so they could eventually secure a full-time teaching job. Even before this, many new teachers were still on the long-term occasional list without the security of a full-time job.

I knew this was the reality of the teaching profession. So rather than becoming frustrated with the system, I decided to create a different goal for myself that would ultimately get me what I always wanted—a full-time teaching job.

I knew getting into our public board would be fruitless, so I decided to focus on applying to private schools. I applied early, before they even posted positions. Instead of waiting to be contacted for an interview, I called the schools and asked for a face-to-face meeting so I could explain why I would be a great addition to their team of teachers.

There were many schools that I didn't hear back from, and most turned me down. It was just as disheartening as receiving all those college rejection letters. I felt like a failure who had made an enormous mistake pursuing teaching.

One day, I received an email from a school, agreeing to meet with me. Finally! I went in to talk to the vice-principal and explained how passionate I was about teaching and what I could bring to the school. She was impressed with my tenacity and offered me a full-time teaching position.

I could have given up; I could have settled for part-time work, but I didn't. I figured out a different way to reach my goal. In life, you have to be prepared to get back up when you are knocked down. Sometimes that next step is the one that leads you to your goal.

Our Actions Determine Who We Are

We all know how easy it is to talk about what we want, but it's another matter altogether to actually *do* and go beyond dreaming. If you ever took a general science class, you might recall Newton's first law of motion: "Everything will stay in its state of rest until an external force causes it to change its state of rest or motion." I always think of this law as a lesson that, unless we take actions, we will remain as we are—static as a stone.

When wanting to make changes in our lives to improve our career, relationships, or overall mental health, we have to decide to take action. If we don't, then change will not come. But when you feel stuck and unsure of what changes you need to take, that first step feels nearly impossible. So, we retreat into inaction. We think, *It's too hard. It feels out of reach.* We find excuses not to act or we simply don't know how to make what we want a reality.

I love this quote by Ralph Waldo Emerson: "The world makes way for the man who knows where he is going." What does this mean? When you take no action in your life, you are living in a stagnant state and simply moving through life with limited control over where you are going. When you have a sense of purpose and know what you want in life, you can begin by taking steps to make that purpose happen. Goal setting helps us to define our purpose and gives us specific and measurable steps to take to get there.

When deciding to change something in your life, the best thing you can do is to come up with a plan of manageable goals. Sometimes when you look at a project as a whole, it can feel overwhelming. The best thing about having smaller goals is that success becomes more visible and attainable. As you complete each goal, you feel yourself becoming more motivated.

Nothing Happens Until There Is ACTION!

As humans we tend to sit around talking about things that need to change, what is wrong and what should be done, but we don't have any action plans in place to make those changes happen. We feel satisfied that we have done something, but in reality nothing has happened. No action has been taken. Nothing has changed.

I believe this is one of the most important things for anyone to realize—it is only action that counts for anything. Thinking, preparing, and talking may be important steps to take before action, but nothing happens without *taking* action. What have you been talking and thinking about that is demanding action right now?

The boldest step I took was quitting my secure teaching job and starting my own business. My husband and I decided we wanted to start a family and assumed it would be easy to get pregnant, but we were wrong. We spent three years trying to conceive, even going through fertility treatments. When we finally got pregnant, I decided I wanted to stay at home with our daughter. Being adopted and not having any genetic family, I always dreamed of having a biological connection to someone. When I finally had my baby in my arms, I didn't want to let her go, even to go to work. I knew this wasn't realistic because my husband and I lived in an expensive city and needed two incomes to make ends meet. So, I decided I was going to try and start my own business, one that I could work on from home.

Business idea number one: My first idea was to sell used clothes on eBay. There were two problems with this plan. The first one was, with the cost of shipping and the low price you must sell the clothes for, it is a very difficult way to make money. The second and more important problem was *I hate shopping* and, honestly, I have little fashion sense.

Business idea number two: The second idea I had was pregnant belly casting. When I was pregnant with my daughter, my husband and I bought some plaster strips at the pharmacy and made a cast of my baby belly. It was a lovely 3D keepsake of what my body looked like then. I figured I could do this for other women. One of my friends was pregnant at the time and agreed to be my guinea pig. I created the cast and quickly realized or, more accurately, remembered that I have zero artistic talent. There were other women doing this professionally who were amazing artists, producing beautiful belly casts, and mine looked like a grade school arts-and-crafts project.

After two failed plans, I may have started feeling defeated, but I didn't give up. So, I started talking to friends, asking them what they thought my strengths were, what I was good at, and what would be a good business idea for me. One of my friends said, "Why don't you start a baby sign language business where you teach other moms to sign?"

Business idea number three: Yes! Of course, why didn't I think of this idea before? I had taught my baby to sign. I was a certified teacher and curriculum expert with a knowledge of American Sign Language. Of course, I could teach other moms how to sign with their babies. Even though I was caring for a newborn, I decided to go to night school to get my American Sign Language and Deaf Studies degree in order to become an expert in the field.

This is where talking and planning are the essential precursors to taking action. A brainstorming session with friends revealed an idea that should have been obvious to me. I set out to create baby sign language classes and developed that business into one of the largest baby signing companies in North America. I wouldn't be where I am today if I hadn't taken action and if I had let little failures defeat me along the way.

Taking Action: Five Simple Steps That Will Empower You and Change Your Life

Imagine this: You are very excited about a new book you found online that claims to hold the "secrets to wealth creation and success." You order it immediately and can't wait to get your hands on it. When it finally arrives, you open it up quickly, intent on devouring the information and making the changes you want in your life. You read the cover blurb and maybe a page or two when, suddenly, your kids start screaming for your attention, or you have to cook dinner, or it's time for the news. Life happens and gets in the way.

Eventually, the book becomes one more thing you didn't follow through on, another opportunity lost, and you become less confident in your ability to affect any real changes in your life. You become a spectator, watching life pass you by. If this sounds familiar, don't get discouraged. Realize that today doesn't have to be like yesterday and the past doesn't determine who you are. Here are the steps to help define yourself:

STEP 1: *Accept responsibility—you got yourself here, there's no one else to blame.*

Unless you recognize that your choices have brought you to this particular point in your life, you will not be able to move forward. Are you taking responsibility for your actions, or are you playing the blame game and becoming great at making excuses? If you find yourself living a life that you neither asked for nor want, now is the time to take responsibility and make a change.

I graduated from a university with a general arts degree, deciding not to continue with a more advanced degree that would open more doors for me. That choice led me to settle for a job that made me unhappy. I quickly realized I would have to rethink that decision in order to move forward in my life. The choice to go back to school wasn't easy. It was time-consuming and expensive, but I was either going to continue to be unhappy or I was going to do something about it.

STEP 2: *Take charge—know what you want and why.*

As simple as it sounds, your life can literally change in a moment. All you need is a strong enough reason that moves you to say, "Enough." That single decision is the first step that will allow you to take definitive action. However, you not only need to define *what* you want, but also be clear on *why*. The reason behind your goal must be compelling enough for you to keep going in the face of adversity. Change requires consistent action until you gain enough momentum to carry you through. This is where a lot of us give up.

When I was working in the office job, I didn't feel fulfilled. My role in the company wasn't giving me a sense of purpose. I wanted to become a teacher because I wanted a sense of purpose. My "what" was to become a teacher, my "why" was because I needed a sense of purpose, and I knew teaching would give me that.

STEP 3: *Take action—set yourself achievable daily targets.*

It is said that the journey of a thousand miles begins with a single step, but I have to add: *in the right direction*. In today's society, it's easy to be too busy being busy. Define your goal and break it down into monthly, weekly, and daily targets. Once you have determined the targets, set yourself two or three tasks daily and work on one at a time without interruptions. This not only ensures better performance, but also the achievement of daily goals will begin conditioning our brains to accept success.

When I finally decided to make the move from office work to teaching, it didn't just happen overnight. I had to make a plan to get from point A to point B and those two points were very far apart. If I thought about just point B, then I would be overwhelmed and may never have taken action to get there. Instead, I broke it down into manageable tasks to reach my goal. An example of those tasks may look like this:

POINT A—STARTING POINT
Task 1—Research my options
Task 2—Make a list of five to ten viable options from the research I did
          in Task 1
Task 3—Write a list of what is required to apply to each college and the
          costs involved
Task 4—Select three solid options to attend open houses and learn more
Task 5—Go to open houses and ask questions
Task 6—Apply to colleges
POINT B—GET A FULL-TIME TEACHING POSITION

There were many tasks between here and reaching my goal. I studied hard, graduated, and wouldn't give up when jobs were hard to come by. By breaking down what you want into manageable tasks, it makes reaching your goal easier and less daunting.

STEP 4: *Believe—for things to change, you must change.*

Learning to master frustration and setbacks is key to our success. It is not about how much you can handle; it is about how you handle it. Next time you feel frustrated, change your focus and don't let it ruin your day.

Thoughts are powerful. If you *think* you can become successful, you can. Simple visualization techniques will allow you to see the results you want to create in your life until they become real. It can be as simple as sitting quietly, closing your eyes, and visualizing the changes you want. The positive results will reinforce your belief of what's possible.

When I first set out to become a teacher, I faced rejection after rejection. If I let those setbacks stop me from reaching my goal, then I wouldn't be where I am today. Instead, I kept adjusting my methods and taking action until I reached my goal. If I had stopped trying, then I'd only be hurting myself. I had to *believe* in myself and continue to fight in order to realize my dream.

Overcoming Self-Limiting Beliefs

You must become aware of what's holding you back, otherwise you will never be able to move forward. Your self-limiting beliefs and perceptions are unconscious. They shall remain nameless, secretly throwing up barriers to your success in the recesses of your mind until you take action. They remain the boogeyman that's hiding in the dark until you shut your self-limiting beliefs down.

I've wanted to write this book for years, but I always thought that no one would be interested in what I have to say. Part of the reluctance was my belief that I wasn't qualified to write such a book. So instead of giving up on this dream, I became qualified. I squashed my self-limiting beliefs by taking action and becoming educated in the field of self-help, which gave me the authority to write the book that I've wanted to create for years.

When you find yourself continuously shrinking from certain tasks, start a journal of your inner dialogue. Perhaps you'll become aware of a sense that you don't want to call anybody because you think the person on the other end won't want to talk to you. Ask yourself, "Where did this belief come from?" and write about it. You might be surprised where these roadblocks stem from in your past.

As a young child, my daughter had a lot of confidence. But when she started high school, she was convinced she wouldn't make any friends because she believed that everyone found her annoying. She had massive anxiety in all social situations and tried to fade into the background. The self-esteem that she once had in spades was squashed. When she started therapy to work on her anxiety issues, she finally realized where they stemmed from. When she was in the seventh grade, a group of girls told her over and over again that she was annoying. She took that to heart and carried it with her for years. She was always surprised when she made friends because she believed no one would like her. It wasn't until she finally started talking about it and evaluating why she felt the way she did that she was able to let her insecurities go.

You may have to journal over and over again. The initial experience of journaling will form neural connections in your brain. Your neural connections are like roads along which your thoughts travel. As long as the old roads exist, your thoughts will travel there. As you are taking action, reframing the old experiences and putting them in their proper place, you are building new neural connections, new roads along which your new thoughts will travel. You'll find that it becomes easier to pick up that phone. Occasionally, the old fear will pop up as an unconscious thought travels down the wrong road. Don't freak out; just make a point to get back on the new road the moment you take notice of it.

Believe in Your Purpose

I always felt like I was put on this earth for something more, but I didn't always know what that something more was. I grew up, went to school, got a degree, started a job, and was incredibly unhappy. What was the purpose of my existence?

When I finally became a teacher, I loved my job and felt incredibly fulfilled. I loved my students and was inspired by their little successes that I had a small part in helping them achieve. Life was good. I felt like I was making a difference, one student at a time.

Then I had my daughter, and I started my baby sign language company. It was nice that I was helping parents learn how to sign with their babies, but the most inspiring moment for me was when I received an email from a mother in another part of the world.

I had posted videos on YouTube of my daughter signing. This mother emailed to tell me she had a two-and-a-half-year-old, nonverbal autistic son. Life was incredibly frustrating because he couldn't communicate with them, and his temper tantrums were getting worse and worse. Finally, one day a friend told her about baby sign language, so she looked it up on the internet. She came across my signing video, and her son overheard my daughter's voice and came into the room to see what it was.

He sat at the computer for forty-five minutes watching the video over and over again and, at the end of the forty-five minutes, he turned to his mom and signed something. This was the first form of communication she had with her son. She was emailing me to tell me that we were angels to her family. We made a huge difference in their lives, one that I had never even imagined was possible.

I felt full, like that was my cake and everything else I did was icing. This was my purpose. To make such a huge difference in someone's life is an incredible feeling. Over the years, I've received similar emails and have loved reading every one of them. However, as much as I love baby sign language, my kids grew up and my interests changed.

At one point, a friend of mine had said I should write a book that tells my story of overcoming adversities. I always thought it was a great idea but believed that no one would really want to hear my story. For years after, I couldn't get the feeling of wanting to share my story out of my head. I desired to help others if I could, to continue on the path to fulfill my destiny and purpose. But still, I couldn't make myself write the book.

When my daughter entered high school, she developed severe depression. I felt terribly guilty because I have depression, so naturally I assumed she got it from me. Seeing your child in pain and feeling responsible is one of the worst kinds of heartbreak.

So, when my daughter started self-harming and wanting to die, that need to share my life experiences with her and everything I have gone through was too big to ignore. I was a cutter; I tried to kill myself. I was depressed and didn't want to exist.

I wished to share all those feelings with her and tell her that life is going to be okay, even when you cannot bear the pain of living today.

That's what made me realize I not only wanted to write this book and share my story, but I wanted to come at it from an area of experience and professional expertise. So I took action to make this book a reality. I went back to school again and got a psychotherapy diploma with specialties in cognitive behavioral therapy (CBT) and dialectical behavioral therapy (DBT) so that I could help my daughter and you.

Your purpose in life may grow and change as you grow and change. You may reach your dream and be content and happy for your whole life, and that is great. However, you may feel the need to change throughout your life, to find a new and different purpose. If you do, remember to always continue to take action to make those things happen for you that you want to have happen. Because if you do nothing, nothing will happen.

Visualizing Your Goals

Referring to your responses to the questions from chapter one, sit down and write some goals. They can be as big or as little as you'd like. By writing down these goals, it will help you to begin working toward them. These goals become tangible, something you can reach if you work hard. I will use my own goal list as an example. I wanted to stop viewing myself as a victim of abuse and to change my thought pattern from victim to survivor. My first goal looked like this:

Goal 1. Stop viewing myself as an abused person who is still suffering today.

Steps to reaching my goal:

1. Every time I start thinking about being damaged because of situations that happened in my past, I will stop and recognize my thoughts. What are my thoughts? Why am I having these thoughts now? Was there something that triggered these feelings?

2. I will ask myself a few questions to help identify my current thoughts and feelings.

   - Are the people who hurt me still in my life? – No.
   - If I allow myself to feel damaged today, am I giving them power in my present life? – Yes.
   - Do they have power if I don't give into those feelings they created years ago? – No.
   - Do I want to give them control over me today? – No.

3. If I let what happened to me in the past guide my reactions, actions, and interactions today, then am I still giving the abuser power over my life today. I will tell myself that I am a survivor, and I am not worthless. I will tell myself they have no power over me now because I am strong, and this is my life, and I control this life. I will refuse to give them power over me any longer. They can't make me a victim today. I am worthy of a happy life.

This may seem silly at first. You may be thinking I'm asking you to tell yourself to cheer up and get over it. I am not. Abuse is a trauma, and it's not something you can "just get over." I am saying that bad things have happened to you, but you have to *actively* stop allowing those bad things to consume your life today and in the future. If we don't try to change the way we view ourselves and any previous trauma, then we won't be able to move on and live happy lives, ones that we deserve. It won't happen overnight, but it is worth putting in the hard work for the path to healing. If you do nothing, then nothing in your life will change.

CHAPTER THREE

Define Your Happiness

> To achieve happiness, we should make
> certain that we are never without
> an important goal.
>
> —Earl Nightingale

Do you remember playing hide and seek as a child—searching and searching until it was time for an afternoon snack? For some of us, this game has never ended. Now, our playground is the entire world. Rather than looking behind trees and in old tractor tires, we search in things, such as love, time, money, marriage, promotions, and other people. This relentless pursuit has now become a desire to find happiness. Although happiness is very skilled at hide and seek, we can find it if we are open to changing how we play the game.

In order to find your happiness, you have to first define it. This is a lesson that seems obvious but is so hard to learn. We grow up believing in a stereotypical definition of happiness. You'll be happy if you get an education, find a good job, make lots of money, get married, own a house, go on vacation once a year . . . blah, blah, blah.

Happiness is not a box or a checklist.

Defining what makes you happy—what you want out of life—will put you on the path to finding happiness. My happiness isn't yours. Your parents' expectation of what your happiness should be doesn't have to be *your* expectation.

So how do you find your happiness?

I have always been a traveler. When I have a trip to look forward to, I'm calm and content. Some people don't understand how much travel impacts my happiness and often judge me for it because what they need is something else.

Happiness looks different for everyone. If exercise makes you happy, then hit the gym as often as possible. If traveling makes you happy, then travel to your heart's content. Live your life doing what motivates you and brings you joy.

Defining Happiness

Too often people are conditioned to believe that certain things will make them happy, when exactly the opposite is true. The Western world is a place full of fast-paced activities and pressure to succeed. We are rarely given any time to think about what happiness might mean to us as individuals, and why we are constantly moving at such a frantic pace. Who has time to think about happiness? We are so focused on what we have decided is important. Happiness has almost been relegated into the luxury category. To expect extended periods of happiness during your lifetime can be perceived as mildly hedonistic.

On the other side of the world, the tiny country of Bhutan

has measured what is referred to as their gross national happiness (GNH) indicator. It is a national measurement taken regularly, much the same as gross domestic product (GDP), and one that is taken seriously by the Bhutanese government. This is a tiny piece of the world that encourages its peoples' happiness and sets it as a defining facet of life.

The mere fact that they take the time to think about whether their citizens are actually happy reflects the values held by the people and concurs with the idea that happiness is necessary for a healthy life.

Following the Bhutanese example, give yourself permission to take time for reflection on how experiences make you feel in the moment. This will guide you toward the direction in which you should move in your quest for happiness.

This may sound ridiculous to some, but many of us go on vacation only to fret about what is happening back at the office the entire time. We have difficulty allowing ourselves the luxury of rest, relaxation, and being in the moment. Guilt and self-flagellation have become incredibly popular in Western society, and the idea that it is possible to fulfill all of your duties and be happy at the same time is difficult for some to swallow.

Go out and explore what it takes to make you happy. Define what happiness is to you on a personal scale. Once you have done this and started to build an idea of what is actually going to move you toward happiness, take one step.

Don't think about how long it is going to take you to get where you are going. Don't think about all of the obstacles that are going to stand in your way. There will always be something to keep you down.

Think only about the first step you need to take until that step is complete. Revel in the knowledge that what you are doing is contributing directly to your future happiness, even if this particular step feels wrong to some part of you. Imagine the happiness that you'll feel when you have achieved your goal.

By the time you arrive where you want to be in life, you may find that it's quite different from the picture you had when you started. As with any personal or spiritual search, the quest for happiness has as many paths as there are humans on the planet, but like every important journey, it begins with a single step.

Define What You Want in Your Life and Find Your Purpose

If you could do anything in your life right now, what would it be? If you were asked to define your purpose in life, could you? If you can't answer either question, you're not alone. People who are able to identify what they want are closer to knowing their life's purpose (or purposes) and are more able to enjoy what they're doing. This is not the majority of people.

This is the experience of a person I'll call Becky, a woman who discovered how unhappy she was with the course of her life—a woman who made the changes necessary to achieve her happiness, even though she wasn't wholly sure what that happiness looked like.

Becky's Story

Becky is fifty-two, vivacious, confident, a mother of two

teenage daughters, and has just changed everything in her life based on the fact that she wasn't living how she wanted, even though her family and friends thought she was.

Becky had always thought she was following the "right" path until she realized that she had no idea what her path looked like, let alone where she was going. Becky was always the person who was in control. She worked in a high-powered job where she was perceived to be successful based on the growth of the business, the caliber of clothing she wore, the amount she felt needed and recognized in her role, and the expectations of what a successful person has, along with what she sounds, looks, and acts like.

As a single mother and a woman, she never said no if something didn't suit her because she needed to feel needed.

One summer, Becky completed a four-month mentoring course for her business. When the course ended, she realized that the business setup and situation she was in was not working for her. Her business partners treated her more like an employee than a partner. Her hours at the office were long and stressful and, more often than not, she took her work home with her. She had no time for anything else in her life, including things that made her happy. She didn't want the business to continue the way it was just to keep her two business partners comfortable.

She was not happy.

Instead of accepting what was expected of her, which would have run her into the ground, Becky decided to simplify her job and her life. She began to create something new for herself, even though she had no idea what it would be, how it would look, or when it would happen.

Becky made massive changes, including selling her share of the business and selling the family home that no longer felt like home. She moved into a city apartment with her daughters and started focusing on her interests and desires instead of making choices she thought everyone expected her to make.

There was a massive amount of freedom that came with the decision to walk away from her business, followed closely by moments of sheer terror and panic at what she had done. These feelings of excitement and dread are to be expected when making huge, life-changing decisions.

It's been over six months now, and Becky has had three or four serious occasions where she felt regret for giving up her business. The move with her daughters to the city has not been as successful as she had hoped, so they're moving to a better location for them. But compared to everything Becky has gained, the doubts and disappointments are very minimal.

Sometimes it's about defining what we don't want in order to find what we do want.

Start with Your Own Small Step

While Becky's story may seem like an extreme example of identifying what you want and making changes in your life to suit your purpose, it doesn't have to involve massive upheaval.

Take ten minutes out of your day to look at where you are now and where you want to be.

1. *Ask yourself these questions:*
   - Who am I?
   - Who do I love having in my life?

- Who and what do I not want to be a part of my future?
- Who and what do I want to be in my future?
- What would I love to be doing more than anything else in my life?

2. *Write your answers down to help you focus on defining your wants.* It's only if you don't know what you want right now. Sometimes, it's defining what you don't want in order to clarify what you do. The first step is starting to define your parameters so you know where you're at right now.

3. *Start with small steps.* Ask people who are doing what you want to do, or living the way you want to live, how they do it. Taking the time to research, question, and think about what you really want is an important step. Breathe, take small, even steps, and allow yourself time to figure out what you want.

4. *Don't feel that you need to make sweeping changes and alter your whole life overnight.* Sometimes we chase and focus on the end result, and that becomes so overwhelming that we end up stumbling and failing or not even taking the first step.

5. *Don't be your own worst enemy.* When we want to make changes in our lives and try to figure out ways to do so, we often become our own worst enemy. Instead of taking action and making changes, we spend so much time with the planning that we never end up getting to the doing. Don't stand in your own way. Think about what you want, what will make you happy, and take the first step to make that happen.

Remember that defining your current purpose is not a grand gesture, even if the outcome results in major changes. Your life purpose can often be defined by what it means for you to relax, be yourself, be in a comfortable position, and not be afraid to explore all aspects of that.

Setting Happiness as a Goal

Goal: Be happy.

You can set happiness as a goal, just as you would for anything worthwhile you desire. To be fair, the process of setting that goal may not be as easy as, say, losing ten pounds or running a five-mile race, but anything is achievable if you break it down into small, manageable steps.

Since happiness is a state of mind and the mind is ever-changing, adapting, and evolving based on our life experiences, our state of happiness is therefore ever-changing. To be clear, achieving and sustaining a constant state of happiness is possible.

How can you set a goal to achieve something that is so abstract? Start by setting a goal to achieve a slightly higher baseline level of happiness than where you are today. According to several research studies, your natural disposition to view the glass as half-full or half-empty is largely dependent on your genes.

In working with depressed patients, Dr. Aaron T. Beck, president of the nonprofit Beck Institute for Cognitive Therapy and Research and professor of psychiatry at the University of Pennsylvania, found that those who are depressed experience what he calls "automatic thoughts." He discovered that such thoughts pop up spontaneously, and the negative thought content falls into three categories: ideas about themselves, the world, and the future. Dr. Beck began helping patients identify and evaluate their thoughts and found that by doing so, patients were able to think more realistically. That led them to feel better emotionally and behave more functionally.

The trick is to catch yourself having the thought, identify it as negative, and then alter the distorted thinking to something more realistic. This requires consistency and a behavioral change. If your happiness baseline is naturally low, you can make it a goal to improve your disposition. It will take effort. Nothing about changing one's mind-set is easy. Goals you are truly committed to achieving and that you believe you can attain will be the goals you most likely will achieve. You must do a minimum amount of work to maintain your new level of happiness. To continue to grow and improve, you will continually be setting new goals.

For a big chunk of my life, I was depressed. I felt sad often and let that feeling of unhappiness consume me. Finally, I decided I didn't want to be constantly blue or depressed. I began by focusing on my days. Each day I would make a goal to be happier and more optimistic than I was the day before. I began to really recognize the thoughts I was having that were bringing my mood down, making me feel sad or anxious. What I found was little things felt huge, and they impacted my emotions negatively. These little things would mean nothing to most people, but they would consume me.

When I lived my life not recognizing what was making me feel down, I lived my life in a state of unhappiness. It always felt like I was unhappy for no reason and therefore depressed. When you have depression, your brain is your own worst enemy. It doesn't allow you to feel better, and its negative thoughts keep you down. Without putting in the work to recognize what is making you feel stressed, anxious, depressed, or simply sad, you will be unable to make the changes needed to start feeling better.

For example, I used to wake up and check my phone before even getting out of bed. Occasionally, I might come across an email that stressed me out or made me feel bad without really recognizing or acknowledging that it did. I would get up and get on with my day feeling down. While getting my kids ready for school, one of them would say or do something that would exacerbate my already-sensitive feelings, without me really acknowledging or recognizing the thing that initially made me feel sensitive. I was consumed with sadness because I let things affect me out of habit. Finally, when I set happiness as my goal, I became aware and present with my emotions. I'd still wake up and check my emails and feel down, but I would stop and think about what made me feel down. When I realized it was an email, I would address the feelings I had surrounding that email. By addressing those isolated feelings, I was able to deal with them and let them go.

Finally, I realized that by checking my emails in bed, I was opening myself up to emotions I didn't need to have first thing in the morning. I began changing my routine. I stopped checking my emails in the morning until after I got my kids off to school. I became much happier, which my kids felt and responded to. One small step toward my goal had a huge snowball effect on the rest of my day.

If you decide to set happiness as a goal, define what success will look like once you have achieved it. This will also help define how your new level of happiness will look and feel. Unless you have a clear vision of what you want, you will not achieve it.

Since happiness is a state of mind, defining it may be the most difficult part of setting this goal. Notice the times in your life when you are feeling happy. Maybe it's after you've had a long conversation with a good friend, once you've finished a weekly yoga class, or maybe while you're cooking. What about those moments or events makes you feel happy? Draw upon these instances in your life where you could honestly say, *I was happy,* and write down what about that experience made you feel that way.

Stop Focusing on the Negatives

Focusing on what your life lacks will not help you reach what you want. When you feel your life lacks something, be it a relationship, a better job, more time, or whatever, negative thoughts come to mind and you think, *If I had [blank], I'd be happy.*

I admit that I used to have those moments quite regularly. It's a terrible mental state to be in because you start to push yourself toward the things you don't really want just by thinking too much about them.

The mind is more powerful than we give it credit for. It's ironic, but by thinking, *If I didn't have this much work, I'd be happy*, you are convincing your mind that you don't deserve to be happy. Your subconscious will make sure you aren't happy until you don't have that much work. You end up convincing yourself that the thing you believe you're lacking is the critical factor that defines happiness for you.

The consequence of this frame of mind is twofold. First, it's a fact: You will not be happy today as long as you're saying to yourself that, to be happy, you need something you don't have. There's no one else controlling your life. It's not the media. It's not your boss at work. It's you telling yourself that you are not happy.

You are choosing to engage in a negative state of mind. You lose the capability to enjoy, and you enter what I call a negative feedback loop. *Because I don't have [blank], I'm not happy. So, I feel bad, and because I feel bad, I see things negatively. It seems people are being unfriendly. It's as if things have turned against me.*

You're waiting for tomorrow without taking any positive changes or steps.

Secondly, because you've tied your happiness to something you don't have, you might assume that even though you're not happy right now, this attitude will push you toward achieving that thing you don't have. That is not true. You haven't told your subconscious what you want. You've just stated the current situation: *I'm not happy because I haven't been promoted yet.* That train of thought doesn't take you anywhere. It reinforces the same idea and allows it to become true in your mind.

You're not happy because you haven't been promoted. Period. No action plan, no goal, no future. Just a present, negative statement.

The truth is, as I've experienced time and time again, there will be a new reason why you're not happy once you get promoted. *I'd be happy if I didn't have to work so many hours.* The negative feedback loop repeats.

I always thought happiness had to do with success, with success defined as being capable of improving yourself over time and getting closer to your greatest potential. I truly believe that as long as you're always pursuing to be better today than what you were yesterday, you'll be happy. I mean "better" in the most profound sense of the word. I believe you are better today than yesterday if today you are nicer to people, more confident in yourself, and so on.

This had always been my frame of mind. But—and here's the big but—it had not made a huge difference in the end. I always came back to the negative frame of mind: *if I had [blank], I would be happier.*

It wasn't until recently that I fully understood:

- *Yes*, it is important we always "fight" to become better individuals today than yesterday.
- *Yes*, there will always be things we're lacking. It's a fact of life!
- *No*, you can't avoid negative thoughts popping into your mind from time to time. It's in our nature.
- A big *yes*, happiness is about finding a direction in life. That's the single, biggest truth in life. Happiness is about purpose.

It's a simple, yet powerful and life-changing concept—we are able to enjoy life and be happy when we have set goals for ourselves. We find happiness when we know where we are going.

I'm sure you've experienced it at some point in your life. Maybe you had a short-term goal at work. Maybe you've studied at a university and found yourself pursuing clear, defined, and measurable goals. Do you remember how you felt during those times? Did you have a sense of purpose?

Give yourself a moment to imagine what you want out of life. Picture it in your mind. Imagine yourself having achieved what you want. I can guarantee you that if you ingrain these goals in your mind, two things will happen:

You'll enjoy the process of pursuing your objectives. You'll be happy today, even if you have to work harder, because you know you're one step closer to where you want to be. This frame of mind puts purpose behind each and every action, each and every day.

You will get there. Don't fall into the trap of believing this is just "positive thinking." Give yourself the opportunity to believe you will achieve anything you set for yourself. Commit to it. Visualize it. Write your goal in ink but your deadline in pencil. If you don't reach a goal when you had expected to, it's not a failure. You will achieve it; you just underestimated the time required to get there. Simply set a new deadline.

I used to find vision boards silly. I didn't get the point. You sit with different magazines and cut out pictures of things you want for your life, then hang a board somewhere where you can add those pictures and see it daily. Eventually your vision board will come true. Nonsense, right?

Now I understand. It's about thinking over what you really want, being mindful of what will make you happy, and having a reminder of it so that you don't forget what you are working toward. You are consciously and mindfully defining your happiness and setting goals to get there.

You don't need a vision board to define your happiness. You do have to sit down and give it thought. Be mindful of where you are in your life and where you want to be. Put aside what you think you should want or what your parents told you that you should want. What do *you* want for your life?

Life Is About Setting Objectives for Yourself

Objectives give you a sense of direction. When I work with my students on creating a "Content Development Strategy," one of the first things we do is set our objectives to obtain our goals. Think of objectives as a map to reaching your ultimate goal. Objectives are specific and measurable. Without objectives, long-term goals can become overwhelming, but by breaking these big goals into tiny, achievable goals, you create stepping stones for yourself to steady the path.

It all comes together in the end. It *does*. My life and yours have unique purposes, yet the same final destination. You and I are both destined to achieve our greatest potential. You and I are destined to become the best we can be.

Don't allow the perceptions of others to cause a "smoke and mirrors" effect on your ability to find true happiness. Many times, people who are the closest to us will express their ideas of how our lives should be. Since we know that it is out of love, we allow their projections to impact our decisions, which lead us in a different direction that may not be in line with our happiness. Only you can define what you want out of life.

By changing how we seek happiness, we move into a much better vantage point for finding happiness. When we stop searching for happiness in outside sources, we redirect our focus to looking in the proper place—ourselves.

Setting and Achieving the Goal

Once you have chosen happiness as a goal and defined what happy looks and feels like for you, it's time to bring the goal to life. Here are six steps to help you start attaining happiness:

1. *Write down your goal as if you have already achieved it:* The idea here is to write down how you will feel once you have achieved

the goal. Example: I am proud of myself for the ability to remain positive and happy even when things around me are challenging.

2. *Add it to your daily to-do list:* Recommit to your goal every day. Over time, what once took a lot of effort to commit to will begin to feel completely natural. There is this thing called the *21/90 rule*. The idea is that it takes twenty-one days to develop a habit and ninety days for it to become a permanent lifestyle change. Commit daily to your goal for ninety days and it will naturally become a part of your life.

3. *Do things that make you happy:* If music makes you happy, listen to your favorite tunes daily. If your dog makes you happy, take time each day to play with, snuggle, or walk your dog. Whatever it is that brings you moments of joy—do it daily.

4. *Post your goal where you can see it:* Read it several times a day. Make it a priority and a habit.

5. *Visualize it:* Reading the words *happy*, *smile*, and *fun*, or seeing pictures of people smiling and doing things you associate with fun, will immediately elevate your mood.

6. *Review and evaluate your commitment to your goal regularly:* Your goal needs to energize you. You will not put the work in to do something if you're not invested. Goal setting requires motivation and personal investment. Ask yourself if you are committed, excited, and energized by your goal. If it is worthwhile, you will find a way to achieve it.

You deserve happiness. Don't deprive yourself of what you deserve.

CHAPTER FOUR

Making Good Relationships Last

A good relationship is when someone
accepts your past, supports your present,
and encourages your future.

—Zig Ziglar

In all of my relationships before my husband, I often felt insecure and jealous. Looking back, I realize my partner did things that gave me a reason to feel that way, and then I grew dependent on him. It's common to think if we make our partners feel they need us, then they will stay.

I'm so glad that my husband showed me that if you support your partner unquestionably, then your partner will want to stay with you because you make them feel secure.

Why would you want to leave someone who makes you feel secure, who always has your back, and who tells you that you can do whatever you dream? If you both treat each other with the utmost love and support, then you'll have a great relationship.

Love isn't always easy. Sometimes you grow apart, but that doesn't mean you won't come back together if you work on it. Don't get mad at your partner when you are experiencing a moment of separation or you aren't seeing eye-to-eye with each other.

Remember that you love your partner and trust you will find balance once more. Relationships are work. Just like a job, you have to go to work and put in the effort to get things done every week. You would never go to work and do nothing until it was time to go home. Think of relationships the same way. You have to continually do the work to make them great.

Successful Relationships Are a Two-Way Street

Enduring love requires learning how to become a loving, caring companion. In the United States, statistics show that about half of marriages end up in divorce. Yet many of the divorced people end up remarrying, and the statistics for those marriages lasting are even worse. These statistics show that long-lasting relationships take work. Relationships have to shift from the early physical falling-in-love stage to caring about growing together.

In a healthy relationship, we must learn to operate on two levels. It is vital for individuals to take responsibility for their own development and, at the same time, learn to care about the well-being of the unit they have formed. Moving from a single person to a couple means having to ask the question, *How will the things I want to do affect my relationship?*

You can no longer simply make choices and decisions based

solely on what you want. Yes, you should make sure to do things that make you happy, and your partner should support you in those decisions. However, it is your responsibility to consider your partner when making life-impacting choices, just like it is your partner's responsibility to do the same for you.

Each person has to learn to think on two levels: about *self* and simultaneously about *the partner*. This is where the process can break down. I have seen in many married couples the tendency to still act single while leaving the relationship growth up to chance.

This does not mean that you lose your individuality within the relationship. My husband and I have different interests. I'm not a fan of going to concerts, but my husband is. He enjoys concerts either alone or with friends. I enjoy traveling so when my husband can't join me, I go with friends. We are secure in our relationship to be individuals because, as individuals, we are still part of a unit, and we always make decisions based on that unit.

It is important for you to maintain your individuality within a relationship. It can be problematic when people get into relationships and are only able to do things together. Sometimes, that can be just as unhealthy as making choices and decisions as a single person within a relationship. You *should* still have individual interests and activities. Just because you are part of a couple does not and should not mean you lose your sense of individual self.

When you're part of a couple and have individual activities and interests, your decision-making that surrounds those activities should always consider the partner. My husband goes to concerts, and I'm completely comfortable with him doing this because I know he isn't going to behave in a way that is detrimental to our relationship. He isn't going to flirt with women. He's going to enjoy the music. When I go on vacation alone, I am still part of a couple, so my decision-making while on vacation always has my husband's and my relationship in mind.

Relationships Take Work

People seem to understand that education, career choices, financial planning, and many other things in life take work. However, they don't tend to recognize that relationships also take work. Many people leave relationships to chance and therefore don't put in the effort that long-lasting, strong relationships require.

When it comes to matters of the heart, I want my relationships to be thunderbolts and lightning, like a fairytale that you see in Lifetime movies. *My lover plants a gentle kiss on my mouth, and my eyes shut, and the next minute, life cuts to me being married, living in the perfect house with the ideal life. The End.* But fairytales don't exist, and in real life, happiness takes work.

Relationships are easy in the beginning when everything is new and exciting. Everyone is on his or her best behavior and is putting his or her best foot forward. It's not until we develop a more secure relationship that we feel comfortable showing our flaws. It's when that comfort level happens that the hard work begins. You won't always have the fire and passion you did when you first started dating. You have to work at keeping that fire alive and, more importantly, look for something better than that fire—security and comfort.

Once you settle into a relationship and the newness fades, relationships begin to feel like work. Things your partner does may start to annoy you where they didn't in the beginning. You each have the challenges of dealing with your own personal theories, worries, limiting beliefs, and triggers that your partner may not understand or accept. There are thoughts, feelings, and experiences from our past that drive our current-day feelings, expectations, and assumptions; each one determines our responses to love and relationships.

Because we are individuals with our own histories, these past experiences often come into play in new relationships. Maybe you've been cheated on and feel insecure, waiting for your new partner to cheat on you. Bringing baggage into the relationship isn't fair to your partner. He or she didn't cheat and may never cheat, but your past experience and those feelings surrounding it will play a role in your relationship if you don't find a way to let them go.

It is unfair and unhelpful to drag negative experiences from the past into our new relationships. This can be especially true for traumatic experiences. There were occasions in my past when my father would lash out and hit me if I did or said something he didn't like. There weren't always warning signs, so I walked on eggshells around him. When I started dating, I would flinch if my boyfriend and I were arguing and he made a sudden move. He would get pissed off that I'd think he would hurt me because he never would have. Yet I couldn't stop feeling the way I did when we argued.

Being part of a relationship means being honest with our partners about things that may trigger us so they can help us work through them. When my husband and I fought and I would flinch, he would gently remind me I was safe with him, that even if we were fighting, he would never hurt me. He wouldn't get mad at my reaction. Instead, he would help me through the feelings I had. My ex's frustration toward me did nothing to help me get over my trauma. He was putting his feelings first. My husband knew the feelings I was having had nothing to do with him and helped me become secure with him. I never had that before in a relationship. This is where the work comes in. You need to work at finding a compassionate balance with one another, where you both feel supported and comfortable.

When someone is reacting to a trigger, it can be hard for the partner to put aside his or her feelings. But relationships take work. They aren't always smooth sailing, and when you or your partner are not willing to put in the work, then it's not meant to be. My husband had to work by putting his hurt feelings aside to help me, and I had to work by hearing his words and accepting them when he would tell me I am safe with him. Over time, I stopped flinching because I was safe with him. We had worked together to become stronger.

Asking for Space to Reevaluate Your Relationship

When a relationship has really broken down, you may want to ask for relationship space. It seems like such a drastic option, and breaking up may seem kinder. Sometimes there is a method to the madness, and taking a break can help you both focus on what is good about your relationship, what needs to change, and what can make it even better.

If you feel your relationship might benefit from taking a bit of a break, it's a good idea to set a few ground rules. Otherwise, there could be a great deal of doubt, insecurity, and uncertainty that overrules reason and good intentions quickly. If you leave things up in the air, your partner might question everything about the relationship and your intentions. Ground rules and deadlines will help eliminate some of this as well. Here are a few great suggestions:

1. Give yourselves a deadline for either reconciling or moving on. While it can be an excellent idea to get a little distance, the line between relationship space and breaking up can become difficult to distinguish if too much time passes.

2. Set up a time for weekly phone calls and place a time limit. This gives you the opportunity to touch base. It's important not to call in between established times without a very good reason, nor is it wise to miss the calls without an equally good reason.

3. Decide upfront if you are going to see other people during this relationship break. It's not good to use this as an opportunity to see if the grass is greener with someone else. If you are going to do that, your partner needs to know and be aware that this is going on. It will be much better than being caught red-handed or even discovered later if or when you get back together.

4. The time apart will hopefully make you realize that, fundamentally, your relationship is good at its core, and by working out the difficulties that brought you to this point, you can come back together much stronger.

My husband and I used to watch the show *Temptation Island*. Couples in long-term relationships who were having issues would go on the show to be tempted into cheating or learn if they would rather stay with their partner. The problem with this show is the unrealistic experiences the couples were having.

It's easy to feel tempted when you've been in a long-term relationship, especially when someone new is paying attention to you and making you feel desired. The issue is that newness will eventually wear off, and you'll be back in a "boring" relationship. If you don't put the work into a relationship, then it will feel stale, and you and your partner will end up resenting one another.

Successful Relationships Need Nurturing

One of the first steps to a successful relationship is to make sure you treat each other with the utmost respect and love. Your partner should be the most important person in your life. From time to time, we all need to conduct a checklist of where our priorities lie. Perhaps you find yourself spending too much time with friends or at the office. This often leads to feeling disconnected in the relationship. If you are guilty of this neglect, check in with yourself and ask why.

Find a time when you focus solely on your partner. This does not necessarily mean you have to run out and spend lavish amounts of money. If you have children, offer to take them out for a couple of hours so he or she can have some quiet time. Even something as simple as serving breakfast in bed or having a hot cup of coffee ready first thing in the morning will do.

There are so many little ways to show your love. Remember when you were dating and you were full of compliments? If you've stopped offering unsolicited praise, be intentional in complimenting your partner or thanking them for things they do. My husband and I have been married for almost twenty years, and he still sends me texts with a heart and queen emoji almost daily to let me know I'm on his mind. I do the same for him to keep us connected and feeling loved.

A breakdown in communication is often the culprit in relationships falling apart. If you don't make an effort to talk with one another, you'll never know what the other person is thinking.

A successful relationship needs nurturing, respect, and consideration of each other's emotions. Without these components, you won't have a healthy relationship. There are subtle ways we fail to show respect, such as forgetting to follow through on a simple request of picking up extra goods at the grocery store or ignoring our partners by not giving them undivided attention when they are talking to us.

Forgetting dates like anniversaries or birthdays is a sure sign that respect has taken a back seat. Sure, we all have things that drain our attention when living busy lives or raising children, but it's imperative to remember things that are important to your relationship.

Set aside one-on-one time. Make sure to check in with your partner to see how he or she is doing. Sometimes we keep our emotions to ourselves and are unable to share what bothers us. If you make time to check in with each other in a meaningful way, then you'll always be able to support one another's emotional needs.

Remember to celebrate your differences. From time to time, we all disagree, but it is how you handle arguments that's important. Don't lose sight of respecting an opposing viewpoint. There is no need to resort to cussing or acts of aggression. Agree to disagree if need be.

Is Jealousy Ruining Your Relationships?

Jealousy is one of the most complex and intense human emotions. It brings out irrationality in everyone and is often born from insecurity. The truth is that most of us will not admit that we are insecure because admitting to this is one of the most vulnerable things a person can do. However, it's something that must be done because if the issue of jealousy isn't resolved, your relationship will inevitably fail. And not just this one, but the next one, and then the next, and the next.

Jealousy, while a natural human emotion, must be tamed before relationships can succeed. Most of the time, a partner is jealous not because his or her partner has done something wrong, but because of a former experience that Partner A has not dealt with.

Are you *too* jealous? Are you constantly checking up on your partner? Are you calling, texting, and/or emailing several times a day to be sure they're where they say they are? Has your jealousy ruined relationships in the past? Do you feel insecure, worried, or angry much of your day? If so, it's time to kick the jealousy habit once and for all.

Realize where your jealousy stems from. If your partner hasn't given you any reason to not trust him or her, then you know it's simply due to your past. Be gentle on yourself. Communicate this past to your partner. If you grew up with toxic parents or have been in other dysfunctional relationships, jealousy and other negative emotions probably feel normal to you. As humans, we're creatures of habit and always more comfortable with what we already know, even if it isn't healthy. Jealousy is simply a learned behavior, and you can deprogram yourself over time.

I had severe jealousy issues in past relationships. I was in a long-term relationship when I was in high school that made me feel incredibly insecure. He was always flirting with other girls in front of me and making me feel like a crazy person when I called him out on it. I grew up feeling insecure, and my feelings led me to men who continued to make me feel insecure. When I finally found a healthy relationship, my insecure brain told me I couldn't trust it.

A therapist once told me that my insecurity was creating a self-fulfilling prophecy. Think of a relationship like a brand-new mattress. You've bought this beautiful and comfortable new mattress that will last you twenty years or more if you treat it the way you're supposed to. The mattress will support you and be comfortable for its lifetime. But if you treat that mattress poorly, constantly jumping on it instead of sleeping, it won't last no matter how great a mattress it is. Don't test your relationship by jumping on it. Treat it with kindness and care, and that relationship will last a lifetime.

Every time the voice of jealousy whispers in your ear, telling you everything you fear most, say "Stop" in your mind or out loud and counter every negative thought with a positive one. Say, for example, your partner is out with his or her friends. Jealousy will pop to the surface, insisting that he or she is cheating on you. You start feeling worried, scared, and angry. Before you pick up the phone to confront your partner, take a deep breath and tell yourself that he or she is not cheating. Fill your mind with positive things your partner has done in the past to show he or she cares about you.

On the flip side, if you have a partner who experiences jealousy, you can help the situation by keeping in touch when you are out, showing him or her that you can be trusted. This is part of putting the work into a relationship. Helping your partner feel secure is just as important as it is for your partner to show he or she trusts you. Working on overcoming jealousy shouldn't be the responsibility of one party. You are a team in a relationship, so act like a great teammate.

Be a lovable person. Jealousy will do all it can to make you feel as insecure as possible, as often as possible. Instead of spending time thinking about how or when your partner will cheat on you or leave you, relax and be the best person you can be. Think about it; he or she would be crazy to have an affair or leave such a wonderful person. Jealousy is pure poison and will eventually kill any relationship.

If you nag your partner or act insecure every time he or she goes out, then eventually your partner is going to become frustrated and fatigued in the relationship. Communicate how you feel, but don't make your partner feel guilty about being away from you.

Take responsibility for your jealousy. Jealousy is a red flag letting you, and anyone close to you, know that you have no control over your emotions and that you expect everyone else to make you feel secure. As of this moment, decide to be the one in charge of your own happiness. You are the one choosing your thoughts and behavior. Nobody can make you feel bad without your permission.

Tame your imagination. Jealousy often gets out of control because our imaginations can run wild and blow things out of proportion. It is important to tame your imagination. The longer you dwell on perfectly innocent situations, the more they seem less innocent. Instead, do a reality check by comparing your obsessive thoughts with what you actually know or have seen.

Jealousy won't just disappear in one day. You have to work on overcoming those feelings.

Work on yourself, inside and out. Many times, we feel jealous and insecure because we're focusing so much on the other person when we truly need to work on ourselves. Maybe you have too much time on your hands and need a job, a hobby, or to volunteer. The better you feel about yourself, the less you'll worry about your partner leaving or cheating.

Taming Your Jealousy

The next time you find yourself getting jealous, I want you to do this exercise. Be mindful of how you're feeling: *I'm feeling jealous because my boyfriend or girlfriend is out with friends, and I think they are going to cheat on me.* You don't know what your partner is really up to when he or she is out with friends. Because you don't really know, you have to trust that they will not misbehave and hurt you. Pick three things that you think they could be doing:

1. He or she is going to meet someone else and leave me.
2. He or she is having a drink with friends and flirting with the waitress.

3. He or she is enjoying a drink with friends and having fun but is looking forward to seeing me later. No flirting, no misbehaving.

Because you don't know for sure what your partner is up to, pick the possibility that feels the best to you. Choose to believe your partner is having fun with his or her friends and is looking forward to seeing you later. By doing this, you are retraining your brain to view your partner in a trusting way. This will help ease those jealous emotions that creep up.

Unlearning jealousy isn't easy, but it's important for living a happy life and being in healthy relationships. Change is hard, but it won't happen without you acknowledging what needs to change and taking the first step to make that happen.

Overcoming Jealousy

First, it is important to understand what causes jealousy, which stems from believing that you may lose your partner to another man or woman. It is a natural emotional response to the fear of losing something important to you.

There are two factors that must be addressed in order to overcome jealousy: *insecurity* and *mistrust*.

Insecurity

A secure relationship won't have jealousy because you are less likely to fear being abandoned when you feel secure.

If you are insecure, sit down with your partner and communicate your fears. You need to seek his or her help with your insecurities without being accusatory in the process. If you come across too strong and demanding, you might make things worse. Here are some things to consider:

1. The actual source of your insecurity—*Core Problem*
2. Options and plans to help manage your insecurity—*Communication*
3. Frequent discussions and updates regarding your insecurity—
    Constant Contact

Insecurity needs to be dealt with from both sides. It won't be done without a free flow of communication and constant contact regarding the core problem that causes these feelings.

People who are insecure are only so because of an innate lack of self-confidence. Putting someone in a situation where they have no experience with it will obviously make them feel insecure. If a man becomes insecure when his wife speaks to another man, even in a business situation, it may be due to a lack of confidence in himself.

Mistrust

Mistrust brings suspicion. Suspicion and insecurity lead to jealousy. If you don't trust your partner, you have an altogether different problem.

Trust is an essential part of the success of any relationship. When you don't trust someone, you will always be suspicious, second-guessing his or her actions, and attributing ulterior motives to everything he or she does.

Is trust earned or given? This is a question that often comes up among couples I've helped in the past. I personally believe that you have to go into a relationship with trust. I think trust must be kept instead of earned. If you don't trust your partner because of bad past experiences, that's not fair to your partner or relationship.

However, you can trust your partner and still be insecure because of past experiences. We don't come into a relationship a blank slate. It would be nice if we could, but the reality is that we are people who have lived lives and experienced things before entering into this relationship. It's those experiences that may make us feel insecure now, even if there is nothing currently to be insecure about.

Trust, on the other hand, is a different beast. If we go into relationships not trusting our partners, that puts undue stress on them from the get-go. Having to earn our trust when they didn't have it to begin with can be exhausting and will breed unhappiness.

Can you imagine if you are in a relationship with someone who doesn't trust you, and yet you've done nothing to break that trust? It wouldn't feel very good, and you probably wouldn't want to be with that person.

If you don't trust your loved one, you need to sit down with him or her and discuss it freely without accusation or argument. No relationship can function without trust and proper communication. It is essential that you can discuss these issues without getting defensive or angry. Trust is best maintained by constant communication and loving discussion of the problem.

Ways to Feel Secure in a Relationship

Giving and getting appreciation promotes emotional intimacy and makes you feel more secure in your relationship. This mutual gratitude increases your commitment to your partner, which also increases the chances of weathering any storms that might come your way.

Are you feeling disconnected from your partner? Do you feel upset and devalued when your partner doesn't appreciate your efforts? Are your thoughtful and considerate actions ignored, but your mistakes highlighted? Your motivation to be close and available to your partner may be at an all-time low. The hurt and bitterness you feel when you are continually unappreciated may blind you to the positives in your partner. Intimacy drops off and the relationship dries up without the original commitment, making separation and divorce a high probability.

It's not too late to turn your relationship around and rekindle the intimacy you once had. You can use the commitment you have left to turn things around.

Recipe for Intimacy

Share your gratitude out loud when you get up in the morning and find your partner alive, healthy, and choosing to be with you. Make a list of three things your partner does for you without you asking and mention each one with genuine thanks at the time they are gifted to you.

In the quiet moments at the end of the day, tell each other how thankful you are to have your partner's loyalty, trust, and patience.

Repeat these daily and mix up the things you are grateful for as you begin to notice more and feel its powerful impact on your well-being.

Forming a Secure Bond with Your Partner

Humans are social animals who desire to form a secure bond with their partners. By secure bond, I mean the sense of belonging and feeling connected to another person. This is the basis for a happy, healthy, and deep relationship. When you have a secure bond with someone, you feel a stronger sense of self that boosts your feelings of competency and self-esteem.

Secure bonds are difficult to build, but they are well worth the reward. Here are some important ways of forming a strong connection with your partner:

Hear each other. Really listen to each other. This might be a small thing to do, but it is very important for building security in a relationship. When you listen to what the other person is expressing, they will feel validated.

Find a common community. Having other bonds outside of your relationship will help you both stay attached to each other. It is important that you have a community you are both involved with outside of your primary relationship. This could be a place of worship, a volunteer center, or your kids' school. Having the support of others that you have things in common with can be comforting when relationships become strained. They can relieve pressure, both for you and your partner.

Accept your partner's uniqueness. Don't wish they were thinner, wealthier, or more romantic. Accept them for who they are and give genuine compliments to show that you really accept them. The more grateful you are for exactly who your spouse is, the happier you'll both be with each other. You don't want to be the partner that is always nagging the other person about how they could look better or act differently. It damages self-esteem.

Become experts at random acts of kindness. Be very intentional about being kind to one another. Learn and then practice the small gestures that say, "I'm thinking of you." How about a cup of coffee in bed, just as they like it? How about a foot rub every now and then or slipping your hand into theirs as you walk down the street? How about a midday text just to say I love you or thank you?

Plan your dates. As we grow more familiar with each other as couples, we often forget the thrill of date nights and let them fall to the wayside. It is important to keep love alive and the bond secure by making time for dates. This can be anything you both enjoy. It could be a movie, yoga, going for a walk, or going dancing. If you have children, planning date nights is certainly harder, but it's even more important. It can be difficult to focus on the relationship when kids are involved. Getting out together even once in a while and not talking about the kids helps keep your romantic bond alive.

Support each other. In this case I don't mean financial support, but rather emotional and instrumental support. Instrumental support is the kind of support that fixes or solves a problem while emotional support has to do with empathetic listening and giving constructive feedback. It's important for partners to find out what kind of support their partner needs and provide it consistently and often.

Find ways to laugh together. I've heard it said that laughter is a spiritual practice that acts as happiness medicine in a relationship. Don't ever allow your relationship to fall into a rut. Remember to do fun things and laugh together. Be silly. Act like children once in a while. If you have kids, put on a silly dance for them. Watch nonsense films together that make you laugh out loud. Just laugh.

Find a healthy way to communicate. Good communication

is a skill that helps deepen bonds. Honestly telling your partner what you need and asking them what they need as well is key. It means asking deep questions to learn your partner's feelings.

Try something new together. Bring some vitality into your relationship by trying something new together. This can be a new sex position or toy, or a type of exercise or activity that neither of you have tried before. The excitement of doing it together makes for lasting memories and a deeper bond.

Always fight fair. Couples argue. It's very important that when you do argue, you both fight fair. Keep your cool during arguments and never interrupt when your partner is airing his or her grievances. When we interrupt others while quarreling, it shows that we are listening to respond rather than understand. It is also important to focus only on the present and not drag in past grievances. Bringing up the past only makes the argument worse. Never ever call your partner names, as you are turning the attention away from the problem and focusing on the person instead. Finally, learn how to apologize as it is usually the quickest way to resolve a conflict.

Consider couples therapy. If you find yourself getting a little distant from each other, try couples therapy. This is particularly helpful if you both have unresolved issues that need to be worked through. Sometimes talking about things with a third party can be easier than trying to work through things on your own. A therapist can help you hear what your partner is trying to say and understand where issues stem from. Problems don't always have a clear-cut source. A therapist asks probing questions to get to the bottom of issues, build a bridge between you and your partner, and foster a stronger bond.

Why Love Is Not Always Enough

Why is it that we have no problem lounging around in our favorite grungy day clothes in front of our partner, but if our friends or coworkers were on their way over, we'd change into something decent in a hurry?

I'm not suggesting we throw away our comfortable clothes, but I am suggesting we look at the curious differences between how hard we try to get others to like us and how many of us in long-term relationships have stopped trying.

Part of the reason we're comfortable in front of our partner is due to a feeling of comfort we build after knowing that other person for a while and feeling secure that they love us, warts and all. That's a good thing and should be celebrated, but let's look at another reason we may not care so much about putting our best foot forward for our partner—we don't feel we need to anymore.

When you were first dating, you weren't only aware of the desire for that special someone—you were mindful of whether or not you liked him or her and whether those feelings were returned. "Like" is a grossly overlooked aspect of long-term romantic relationships and the missing ingredient for many couples who report they've "fallen out of love" with their significant other or they love their partner but are no longer "in love" with them.

You have no trouble making sure your friends like you and want to hang out with you. Shouldn't you try to maintain that for your relationship?

When You Stop Liking Your Partner

When a marriage becomes distressed, it can feel as if you still love your spouse or partner but that you're not in love with him or her any longer. I've observed a pattern for some of these couples that might be summarized as: *While I still may love you, I'm pretty sure I don't like you anymore.*

Falling out of *like* with your spouse can pose a significant challenge to your relationship. When you like someone, you want to be around that person and spend as much time as possible with him or her—and the opposite is true when you no longer like someone.

Couples who no longer like one another:

- Avoid each other whenever possible.
- Experience more negative emotions when together.
- Become less tolerant of each other's shortcomings.
- Pull back emotionally and stop sharing the deepest parts of themselves with one another.
- Can begin to feel trapped in the marriage or relationship.

For many couples, continuing to act in ways that will keep *like* alive doesn't fall under the commitment umbrella, but it absolutely should. After all, don't you want your partner to continue to like you?

Think back to when you first started dating your spouse. In the *wooing* stage, you probably acted in ways to capture his or her love. You understood the importance and power of getting your partner to like you.

You should aim to keep the likability factor alive and well. This doesn't have to be a complicated, exhausting process. In fact, the simpler, the better. To create a personalized likability plan for your marriage or relationship, ask yourself the following:

1. What did you do early on in the relationship that helped you woo your partner?
2. What is your partner drawn to about you, and does he or she still find these traits appealing? (If you're uncertain about this, ask him or her.)

Reflect on these questions—your responses will give you important information that can guide you. For instance, if one of the things your partner was drawn to was your sense of humor (and over the years of domesticity, this has been lost), then take necessary steps to bring humor back into the relationship mix.

Seven Keys to a Lasting Relationship

In the romantic journey, we're all looking for basically the same thing—a long-term, successful, secure, and loving relationship. I have found that the following keys have been instrumental to the success of many lasting relationships:

1. *Love unconditionally.* Don't put restrictions or conditions on your love. Allow your love to flow from the deepest place in your heart without expecting anything in return. Unconditional love is love without limits.
2. *Spend quality time together.* Nothing can substitute the time you spend with your partner. Spending time together strengthens your bond and nurtures your relationship. Engage in activities that bring about closeness. Don't let work, children, or outside activities take you away from time together as a couple.

3. *Be forgiving.* A relationship cannot be successful without for-
    giveness. When you are unable to forgive, you harbor feelings
    of anger, resentment, and disappointment. When you let go of
    ill feelings, you free up space to experience more love, joy, and
    happiness. Forgiveness is not forgetting, and it's not allowing the
    other person to get away with anything. It is knowing that humans
    make mistakes, and forgiveness is love.

4. *Communicate effectively.* Say what you mean and mean what you
    say. Never assume your partner knows what you think or feel. The
    only way to be certain is to say so. Don't pretend to like something
    out of fear of hurting someone's feelings.

5. *Maintain honesty.* Trust is the glue that binds relationships
    together, and honesty breeds trust. If you start out being honest
    about the small things, it will be easier to tell the truth about the
    big things. Lying and deceiving leads to the destruction of a rela-
    tionship. Choose truth over fear.

6. *Be accepting.* Acceptance is allowing our partners to be them-
    selves despite their weaknesses or shortcomings. Keep in mind
    that you cannot change another person. We all have quirks and
    imperfections. Allowing people to be who they are can increase
    feelings of love and appreciation.

7. *Keep passion and romance alive.* Passion is what keeps the
    romantic fires burning. Like most things, passion has to be fed in
    order to survive. Keep passion alive with simple acts such as daily
    hugs and kisses, kind words of affection, and compliments. Let
    your partner know that you still find them attractive and desirable.
    A gentle touch goes a long way in showing your partner that they
    are special to you.

Falling in love is magical. We expect it to last forever, but when the magic of falling in love starts to fade and the daily grind of life takes over, problems creep in and communication breaks down. Mistrust increases, resulting in make-or-break issues. *Knowing* that relationships are work and you have to put effort into maintaining them is one step toward a healthy relationship.

CHAPTER FIVE

Toxic Family

> It's one thing if a person owns up to
> their behavior and makes an effort to change.
> But if a person disregards your feelings,
> ignores your boundaries, and continues to treat you
> in a harmful way, they need to go.
>
> —Daniell Koepke

Toxic family relationships can be the trickiest to navigate. Blood is thicker than water, right? I have met many people who have a family member that makes them feel worthless, but they justify their behavior because they are family.

Family is forever, but in some cases, family can be detrimental to your peace of mind, sanity, and well-being. If your life will be happier, healthier, and more peaceful without certain family members in it, this is a sure sign you need to cut them out of your life.

It can be very difficult to face the fact that a family member is causing you so much pain, stress, and anxiety that you can no longer meet them on common ground. I would encourage you to do all you can to repair family relationships, especially if the family member causing the hurt is willing to change.

The familial relationship may, however, be irreparable if certain behaviors are at play—overreacting to the littlest things, manipulating, criticizing, blaming, and lying. A toxic family member may also constantly invalidate or ignore your feelings, undermine your relationship with other family members, and be the one who always seems to be the cause of unwanted drama in your life.

He or she might engage in passive-aggressive behavior, such as criticism disguised as a compliment, the silent treatment, or deliberate avoidance of things you might ask of them. He or she might also refuse to see things from your perspective, choose to never compromise, and won't think twice about yelling, cursing, or calling you names.

A toxic family member may belittle your values, beliefs, and choices; speak ill of you behind your back; make unreasonable demands of you; and be unavailable to help you while expecting you to be at their beck and call.

They may also play the victim with you and threaten suicide or self-harm in order to get their way. They may have volatile or unpredictable moods and behaviors, and create so much stress, anxiety, and pain that your health, ability to work, or general well-being are negatively impacted.

If a family member exhibits most of these behaviors toward you and makes no effort to work on themselves or change their toxicity, you need to leave.

Don't feel guilty about it or remain tied down by family

loyalty. You don't need to make further excuses for abusive family members, like "She doesn't know any better" or "That's how he was raised."

My brother was a toxic family member. He had a horrifying childhood and turned to drugs, alcohol, and criminal activity as a form of escape. It was a lifestyle filled with repetitive crime and prison sentences, and he didn't have an education or any work skills to help pull him out of the cycle. I wanted to do everything in my power to help him, but at what cost? I couldn't help him if he didn't want to change.

Every time I was around my brother, my life would take a nosedive. He sucked me into his self-pity and unmotivated life. He was an alcoholic who would get angry and violent at the drop of a hat, like a bomb that you were never sure when it was going to explode. He wanted things to come easy for him and didn't want to put the work into changing. I let him pull me down more times that I can count.

When my mom finally left my father, my brother was in a juvenile detention center and I felt guilty. I kept thinking, *She took me and left him.* When he was released from juvenile detention, he was sent to my father, who told him over and over that he was unwanted, that my mom left him behind and took me, and that she didn't care about him. This was a severe form of emotional abuse that kept my brother under his thumb by making him feel worthless and unwanted. It's hard to succeed in life when you feel abandoned and that you have no value.

I lived with this guilt for a long time and allowed myself to be manipulated and used longer than I should have. Don't get me wrong, my brother loved me. He probably loved me more than anyone else in his life, but, after life with my father, he didn't know how to let all the negativity and toxic behavior go.

Was it my job to stay with him and let him keep dragging me down? He drained my energy and caused me to lose other relationships in my life. It was an incredibly hard and painful decision to make, but ultimately, I had to take care of myself first. People will say that is selfish, but if I had given my all to him and lost myself, I would've had nothing left to give anyone else. How is that selfish?

The most painful part of this might be that we still love our family, despite all the pain and problems they've caused, but love isn't always enough to make a relationship work. It's a hard truth to swallow.

I applied my mother's advice about a relationship being a building to my relationship my brother. I imagined I was on the tenth floor of a building and my brother was in the basement. I was more than willing to meet him on the fifth floor, but I couldn't keep going to the basement to help him, especially if he wasn't willing to do any work to help himself. I was so torn about not being there for him until I realized I wasn't necessarily ending our relationship. I was putting boundaries up to protect myself. There were times that I gave him all my energy because he had been my protector, and I felt like I owed him something. I then realized that I couldn't constantly make up for the past by sacrificing my own mental well-being.

I knew I had to put boundaries on our relationship, identifying what I would and wouldn't do for him. I told him I was willing to help him find training programs he could attend, but I wouldn't give him money. I'd give him my love and my time but not my money. When he got out of jail, I let him stay with me for a few weeks, but he couldn't move in permanently. And when I wasn't at home, he had to go somewhere like the library or mall as he had stolen from me in the past and I didn't trust him to be alone in my home. I'd help him pay for first and last month's rent, but I wouldn't sign my name to his lease or be responsible for paying his rent every month.

I wanted to help him, but I had been burned before, so I knew the importance of protecting my own mental health by setting up these boundaries. I told him I'd meet him on the fifth floor because I knew he couldn't make it all the way to the tenth. I refused to be sucked down into the basement every time he needed me. I was willing to give him some of my energy but not all. Boundaries are good. They are a necessity in any relationship, especially in an unhealthy one, so don't ever feel guilty about putting them in place to protect yourself.

Toxic Parents

I have firsthand knowledge of dealing with a toxic parent. Growing up, everyone thought my family was normal and my parents wonderful. I was just part of another family down the block. We all did a great job of hiding what was really going on behind closed doors.

I think many of us do this; we don't want the world to see our blemishes. Scrolling through Facebook, we see how most people share mostly positive photos and news. We don't often share the low points in our lives, especially if we find them embarrassing.

My father was a master manipulator as well as physically,

mentally, and emotionally abusive. He, of course, would never admit to any of this. When he strapped us until we formed welts, he believed it was for our own good, helping us understand our errors and making sure we didn't do it again.

My brother and I grew up in fear we would do or say the wrong thing and receive a beating (or "parenting" as my father referred to it), or one of his famous three-hour lectures at the table with his belt rolled up at his side. Whenever we said anything he didn't like, he would put his hand on his belt to show us he had the power. If he didn't like our responses, he would unroll that belt faster than the eye could see and unleash its bite on our bare skin. We lived in constant fear of being hurt.

Growing up, it was the physical abuse I feared most, but it was the emotional abuse he inflicted that played a greater role in the trauma I carried with me into adulthood. He would say things to make us feel like less than we were. I was adopted at birth. We may not share the same blood, but in all rights, I am his child. I've never known any other father. Despite this, he always made it clear that he didn't really want us. He would tell us he agreed to adopt us because my mom wanted children, that he would have been happy not having any. He'd constantly say things to us that made us feel worthless and unwanted. Publicly, he always hid how he truly felt about me for my whole life, and no one knew the brutality that went on behind closed doors. It was only at my wedding reception that his feelings toward me were publicly displayed for all to see.

My whole extended family was there, along with a handful of my closest friends. When it was time for speeches, he stepped up to the microphone and began by saying what a good person he was for plucking me from the *trash* and giving me a better life. Now look at me. I had accomplished what I did in my life because of him.

I almost couldn't believe that he stood up in front of everyone and referred to me as trash. He believed that my birth parents threw me away like garbage, and he rescued me like the hero. My friends and family were shocked. I was not. This was the type of treatment I received from him my whole life.

My mom, on the other hand, was a saint. She was a victim just as much as me and my brother. I was so grateful when she finally found the courage to leave him and relieved not to have to live fearfully every day in an abusive home anymore. However, I wasn't able to cut him out of my life until years later after I did a lot of work on myself to find the strength to say, "No more."

We are raised believing we are supposed to love our parents no matter what. The reality is that we shouldn't have to love someone or stay with them when the relationship is harmful, no matter who they are. We deserve to be happy, loved, and respected, especially by our parents. You are the one in charge of making sure you surround yourself with people who love and respect you.

As hard as it is to end a familial relationship, sometimes it must be done. You don't always have to completely cut the ties like I did with my father. You can put boundaries and limits on it first, but if that doesn't work, then it's time to sever the relationship.

When I was twenty-two, I finally had the strength to put limits on my relationship with my father. I told him that when we spoke or saw each other he couldn't do x, y, and z—the things he did that I felt were manipulative and unfair. I said if he would agree to my boundaries, then I was happy to try to have a healthy relationship with him. If he was unable to do this, then *I* would be unable to have a relationship with him. He agreed.

The very next time we spoke, he broke the agreement and tried to manipulate me. I told him that was the final straw. I had to end the relationship and told him not to contact me again. I wanted a dad who would love and support me. He could never be that person. I hung up the phone and haven't spoken to him since. I miss having a dad, but I don't miss him. He was never my dad. He may have been my father on paper, but he was never my *dad*.

How to Cope with Toxic Family Members

Set boundaries. Even if you're dealing with a person who knows no boundaries, it's important that you try. If said person shows up at your door without calling first, you can choose to not answer the door. If you let that family member in, you are letting him or her know that this behavior is acceptable. It will not help them change. By not engaging in behavior that you disagree with, you let them know that they are not in control. It'll take time for them to realize this and for some, it will be a constant battle. Stay strong, and you'll survive.

Don't give certain family members every detail of your life. They don't need to know what you are doing every minute of every day, nor do they need to know why it took you more than ten minutes to return their phone call. If you are dealing with a "persistent caller," don't call them back right away. Let them wait a day or two and then return their phone call. When they ask why it took you so long to call them back, tell them that you were busy, then change the conversation.

Don't let them guilt you into getting their way. Using guilt is manipulation at its best. One thing to keep in mind when the guilt sets in—the person doing this does not respect you. People who respect others do not use manipulation tactics to get what they want.

Escaping the Severely Toxic Family

Personal change is difficult not only because our core beliefs resist change, but also because systems are resistant to change. Families are systems.

Imagine that after working with a psychotherapist for some time, you've gained renewed confidence, a strong sense of self-esteem, and the ability to deal with issues. Thrilled with your own success, you're eager to bring to others your newfound joy at living. You attend a family dinner and find that the same relatives who used to belittle and demean you continue to do so. To your shock and disappointment, you find that you still resent this ill treatment. Wasn't therapy supposed to make you immune to their criticism? It almost feels as though they were deliberately trying to bring you back to your former state of poor mental health.

Consciously or not, that's exactly what they are doing. Systems resist change, and family systems do everything they can to restore equilibrium. By undertaking psychotherapy to bring about change in yourself, you unwittingly brought about a change in the system. The system will strike back.

Having experienced change in yourself, you want to change others. Unfortunately, that's not the way it works. It's like the old joke—"How many psychotherapists does it take to change a light bulb? Only one, but the light bulb has to want to change."

Despite your best intentions, you can't change other people. In the worst-case scenario, they can sometimes undo your hard-won progress. If permitted to, a system will bring you back to a state that embraces the old, unhealthy you. It is very difficult for an individual to hold out against the continuing pressure and very unlikely that the individual can singlehandedly change the psychology of the group.

Leaving a painfully toxic family situation can feel like crawling out of a slime pit. While your therapist fosters and encourages your liberation, members of the family grasp your legs and try to pull you back. Once you have extricated yourself, don't fall back into the slime pit. Seek new friends, form new networks, and engage in new social situations. It may not be necessary to renounce your family completely. You might be able to safely interact with some relatives one-on-one, but judge the relationship the way you would judge a friendship. Does being with this person make me feel good about myself? If not, better to avoid the relationship. Over time, you may be able to attend family functions or see individuals and not be triggered or negatively affected by their inappropriate behavior. You may clearly see the dysfunction, realizing that you are no longer as vulnerable as you were and cannot be drawn back in.

Don't expect your family members to understand or wish you well when you walk away. Don't make your new, healthy life contingent upon their acceptance, for you'll probably never get it. Consider how much work you put into improving your mental health and whether you want to sacrifice that to a misguided sense of family loyalty. It is not egotistical to put your own self-interest first; it is an essential element of having a healthy sense of self-worth. Taking care of yourself does not equate to selfishness. If you take anything away from this chapter, please know that.

Controlling the Relationship

You are in control of how you are going to allow people to treat you. You need to figure out how you want to be treated and teach others what you will and will not accept from them. Sometimes there is no getting through to family members who treat you poorly. If you try to address your concerns with them and nothing changes, then it is okay to put limits on or end the relationship. Sometimes we think we are doing all we can to change a relationship, but when we really stop and look at it through a non-emotional lens, we realize we probably aren't.

I want you to try this exercise:

1. Write on a piece of paper the name of one family member whose treatment of you you'd like to change. You might have more than one family member this applies to, but I want you to focus on just one individual for this exercise.
2. Write down what you would like to change about the relationship.
3. List a few examples of things that have happened that have upset you and demonstrate their poor treatment of you.
4. Using the list from number three, give examples of how you wish that person had handled the situation differently.

5. Moving forward, how would you like to see your relationship with
    that person change? What do you need from that person?

Writing your feelings on paper can really help to solidify
your understanding of the situation and what you would like to
see changed. Certain things can remain hidden in our minds,
but actually articulating those feelings can give you the power
to make changes.

6. Now, this is the hardest part of this exercise. I want you to tell the
    person how you feel and how you would like your relationship
    to change. You can start by saying that you are bringing this up
    because you love them and you want them in your life, but you
    aren't happy with the way they treat you. You can either do this
    in person or through an email. Some people find it easier to get
    things out in writing rather than face-to-face. Be prepared that the
    person will probably not be happy about this discussion. They may
    feel defensive. If you prepare yourself for this ahead of time, it will
    help you manage your expectations.
7. Give your family member time to digest what you've asked. Try not
    to get defensive and angry. If the conversation seems to be going
    off the rails, then step away and try again when that person has
    had time to ruminate on what you are asking.

Put a time limit on seeing that change happen. Maybe give
the person four months to learn to respect your feelings. If
nothing has changed after that, you will want to revisit this and,
if necessary, end the relationship.

What I want you to do with this exercise is protect yourself. Protect your feelings and create expectations for yourself

about how you want people to treat you. You can't control other people's actions, but you can control your decision to let their actions affect you. If they won't change and they continue to hurt you, then you do not need to accept that. And please understand, you are not being selfish by walking away. You are taking care of your own mental well-being. If you don't do it, who will?

Cutting Ties

Here are tips for cutting ties with a toxic family member:

Acknowledge that this relationship is abusive. This is perhaps the most important, hardest step for many people. Because we love this person or these people, we minimize how bad the situation is and often deny the harm that they have caused. It is very important that you let yourself see it for what it is—abuse.

Don't delude yourself that they will change. Toxic people hardly ever change. If you have given this person enough chances to change and they haven't, odds are they never will. It is imperative that you give up the fantasy that they might; it's what has kept you tethered to them for so long.

Cut the cord. While there isn't a one-step, fix-all solution for the process of cutting ties with a toxic family member, I often promote a phasing-out approach. It's more effective than a slam-the-door-shut-and-walk-away kind of approach. Avoid contact with this person as much as possible and keep your interactions brief when you have no choice. Stop forcing the warmth and care.

Pick a deadline and stick to it. Give this relationship a deadline. This can be a week, a month, two months. During this period, assess your relationship to see if it is salvageable. If it's not, practice self-love and walk away. Tell this person why you can no longer be around them and that you are choosing self-love, self-care, and self-respect over being family.

Deal with family fallout. It is important to be ready to deal with any of the fallout that might come along with ending a toxic familial relationship. You may want to take the time to communicate your feelings and reasons with other family members. Be honest and let them know that you made this decision, not out of malice, but because of a need for self-preservation. Some will believe you and respect your decision. Unfortunately, some will not.

Grieve the loss. You loved this person; it's important that you give yourself the time to grieve over never having the kind of relationship you wanted with this person. Grieve the loss of never experiencing the parent/grandparent/sibling that you needed and deserved.

Get a support system. Get support from a therapist, a support group, or from a friend who's experienced similar issues with a family member. Take this time to focus on the healthy relationships that bring joy into your life.

Ending a relationship will never be easy, and no one said it would be. You may hurt the other person, and knowing that can, in turn, hurt you. Most people don't expect the hurt of being the one to end the relationship, and they are often crippled by the pain that comes with it. The truth is that you will hurt because you are stepping into unfamiliar territory, even if the familiar you knew was a toxic one.

You will miss this person, but the good news is that you will move on and be better for it. Remind yourself why you should do away with that unhealthy relationship:

- Being in bad company is worse than being alone and can be more detrimental to your mental health than being by yourself.
- An unhealthy relationship will stand in the way of your personal growth because you are constantly browbeating yourself.
- Getting out of an unhealthy relationship makes room for a healthier one.
- Cutting ties from a toxic person shows inner strength. If you've had a family member repeatedly tell you that you couldn't last a day without them, this is the time to show them that you have the inner fortitude to do what's right.
- A toxic relationship isolates you emotionally and socially, and may cause physical illness, anxiety, depression, or suicidal ideations and actions. Walking away may be the best thing you will ever do for your mental health.

Severing ties with a family member may be one of the hardest relationships to end. It does not feel natural to end a family relationship. One of the most prevalent mantras in society is that "nothing is more important than family." However, too many family relationships are toxic, and people don't realize they have the choice to cut unhealthy relationships from their lives, even if they are family. No one should make you feel like garbage. No one has the right to take away your self-esteem, self-confidence, and self-worth. Not even if they share your blood! It's okay to walk away.

CHAPTER SIX

Toxic Romance

> Letting go means to come to
> the realization that some people are
> a part of your history, but not
> a part of your destiny.
>
> —Dr. Steve Maraboli

A toxic relationship is characterized by an imbalance of power in which one partner uses physical, mental, or emotional manipulation to ensure that they always have their needs met, often at the detriment of the other person.

Often when we think of abusive relationships, we immediately think of romantic partnerships. While this is undoubtedly a problem in modern society, toxic relationships are not limited to romantic partners. They also include friendships, family, and working relationships—any situation where one individual abuses the bonds with another has the potential to be toxic.

Looking back on my life, I experienced a number of toxic relationships that I allowed to go on longer than I should have.

I've had friends who made me feel guilty for wanting to spend time with other friends. I've had bosses who treated and talked to me inappropriately, not only as an employee but also as a human. I've even had to cut family members out of my life because the relationship was causing me physical and emotional distress.

I'm sure you can think of a few toxic relationships from your past. Pick one of those relationships and think about what made it toxic. If you could talk to your younger self, what would you say? It's easier to see what we could have done differently when we are no longer in the situation, and we can't blame ourselves for that. We grow and learn. Taking a moment to evaluate those past relationships and what you would have done differently is key to preventing those same mistakes again.

If we don't evaluate our failures and change from them, we're destined to repeat those mistakes. Often when we leave bad relationships, we want to erase them from our memories. However, identifying and knowing what was dysfunctional about those relationships will help you create healthy boundaries in the future.

Throughout the next few chapters, I will provide skills to help identify toxic relationships and either eliminate them from your life or recover your power so that the relationship is balanced and healthy.

One of the most toxic relationships is the one controlled by emotional manipulation. Physical abuse is extremely detrimental, but it is much easier to identify than the former. This makes it easier to stay, not realizing the damage they are doing to our psyche.

There are several common characteristics in a toxic relationship.

1. Partner A is always in control of the relationship. He or she decides where they go, when they get there, and what they do.

2. Partner A makes sure that his or her demands are met using physical or verbal abuse, the threat of physical violence, or mental and emotional manipulation.

3. Partner B feels powerless to confront or contradict the one in power. The relationship is a one-way street, with the person in control receiving everything in the relationship. The powerless individual may find his- or herself acting out in uncharacteristic ways due to feelings of helplessness and lack of control.

4. Interactions of this sort often leave Partner B feeling emotionally and physically drained. There may be a component of fear as he or she tries to avoid angering the person in control. Fear of retribution, once it's passed, leaves one exhausted.

I challenge you to take stock of your life. Where can you reclaim your emotional wellness? What aspects of your life need a detox?

Romantic relationships are most commonly associated with toxicity and abuse.

In a healthy relationship, you're comfortable enough around the other person to completely be yourself. You don't have to change to please that person, and honesty is easy. The relationship is built on communication, respect, and mutual support.

In a healthy relationship, there is trust. A healthy relationship makes you feel safe, emotionally and physically, because you know that this other person has no ill intent toward you. This is not to say that a healthy relationship is a perfect relationship. Perfection is not real.

Arguments are an inevitable part of commitment with someone. Disagreements give us the chance to explore different perspectives and help us express our feelings. However, it is never okay for arguments to lead to physical violence. If this is happening in your relationship, this is a serious red flag.

Another aspect of an unhealthy relationship is when the other person has complete control. He or she tells you what to do, humiliates you, constantly checks in on you, or uses threats to make you do what they want. An unhealthy relationship is an unpredictable one. One day, you are happy with this person, and the next, you feel like you are walking on eggshells because you don't know what might set the person off.

When you find yourself in a toxic relationship, it zaps your energy and drains you emotionally and physically. You work and work to try to make it better. Maybe you have gone to counseling together. Perhaps you have stuck it out for so long, hoping that it will eventually get better, and it hasn't. If you have done all this and it's still not working out, it is okay to leave.

I wrote this book with the intent of helping people repair their relationships where the relationships are repairable. However, it is also important for me to encourage people to leave when the relationship is doing more harm than good, especially if your personal safety is at risk.

As you journey with me in this book, I hope that you will find the courage to work on your good relationships and the strength to walk away from the bad ones.

I was married once before my current husband. In my early twenties, I went backpacking in Australia. I'd spent my first year of university taking care of my mom after she had some major health scares. I was alone without help, caring for her, the house, and her finances, worrying that she might die. All of this occurred while attending university and trying to maintain my grades. I needed to get away and take care of just me.

While backpacking, I met this very charming Australian man and fell in love. I wanted a change—an escape—and I found one in him.

After we married, I moved to Australia and life was great for a while. Then things started going downhill quickly. We had to move out of three apartments in a short period of time, and I never understood why. He told me it was because he found a better place for us. They were never better. He worked temporary jobs and always had "business ideas" he was working on. I always supported him, but it never felt like we were moving forward in our adult lives.

Do you ever have that feeling when someone is lying to you, but you can't prove the lie? You feel a little crazy, and when you confront the person, they convince you that you *are* crazy. This was my relationship. One day it finally came to a head when I discovered his gambling addiction. We had to keep moving from place to place because he never paid our rent. He took care of our bills because I worked full time, and he had the spare time to manage our finances.

When I finally discovered his gambling problem, I was devastated. I grew up surrounded by addiction, and I couldn't believe I chose a man with an addiction. I knew firsthand how horrible this disease can be and how it can tear people apart. I remember talking to his mother about it. I was in tears. She also was in tears. She knew what it was like because her husband had also been a gambler, and it nearly destroyed her. It would have if he didn't die early in life.

She encouraged me to leave him—his own mother. She lived it and knew the struggle I would face, and she didn't want that for my future children.

I was so torn about my decision to leave. I loved him, but I didn't want that life. I wanted *him* but not the *addiction*. I tried to stay. We went to counseling, but he wouldn't admit to having a gambling addiction. He said it was simply a problem, one that he could control.

I asked him to move back to Canada with me. I wanted a new life, a different life, a happier life. I wasn't going to get that in Australia where there was easy access to gambling machines. He refused to come with me. This was when I started to realize that our relationship wasn't balanced. He wasn't ever going to put me first.

But still, I told him I would stay if he would go to Gamblers Anonymous. He refused. If I stayed and brought kids into our marriage, then whatever hardships we would face would be because of me. Because I stayed.

I had to make the choice to take care of me, and it was one of the hardest decisions I've ever made. I was going to be a twenty-two-year-old divorcée. Everyone judged me for marrying young, and they were right. It is a horrible feeling knowing that you are returning home to people who think you're a loser who makes terrible decisions.

There will always be people who tell you that you're doing the wrong thing. There will be people telling you that you should stay and work it out. You made a commitment, and it should mean something. But here's the thing. If there are two people who made a commitment, why is the responsibility on *you* to make sure the commitment works? You should do what you can, what is in your power. But when you've done all you can, it's not up to you to do more. The other person needs to play a role, too.

Remember my mom's advice about setting boundaries in all types of relationships? Pretend your relationship is a building. You are on the tenth floor, and the other person is in the basement. When you need to discuss and decide things, you meet on the fifth floor—the halfway point. You are both making equal effort.

If the person refuses to meet you, then you have to walk ten flights of stairs to discuss an issue. You are exhausted and your partner is rested, holding the control. You are in his or her space. You had to make all the effort and sacrifice. It's okay to have to do this once or twice. Sometimes your partner isn't capable of making the climb. But when you are constantly making the climb, the balance is compromised.

In relationships, it's important that you have a balance of power and respect. One person can't give all the time without getting anything in return. You can't have a healthy relationship if you are the one to always give, give, *give*.

People who judge you for making a hard decision don't know how many stairs you've had to climb. They won't always have your best interests at heart. People will judge. Don't let their judgment make your decisions.

It would have been a bad decision for me to stay with my first husband. I wasn't making a bad decision when I left, nor was I making a bad decision when I married him. I loved him. He loved me. It was my decision. So was leaving. I needed to be okay with that, to be okay with being judged by people. They are not the ones who have to live my decisions.

As it turned out, leaving him was the best decision I could've made. I came home and married a man who loves me more than any human on earth could. We have been together for twenty years, and each day he makes me feel loved. We have two beautiful children who live in a safe and secure environment. Life is better than I could have ever imagined it would be, and that's because I made the decision to love myself first.

Improve Your Relationship by Taking Care of Yourself First

It's crucial for you to take care of yourself before trying to take care of anyone else, including your relationship. The old saying "you can't give away what you don't have" rings true. Until you are balanced and happy, you won't have a balanced, happy relationship.

If you skip over yourself and jump immediately into the murky waters of your troubled love, you are at high risk of sinking. Before you confront core relationship issues, first follow these two steps to increase your chances of success:

1. Commit to being okay no matter what happens.

Make yourself a promise that you are going to take good care of yourself and be okay no matter what happens in your relationship. If your happiness solely depends on your partner being a part of your life, then you'll feel fearful and powerless. You'll be more likely to fall into ineffective behaviors, such as begging and pleading with your partner.

This kind of behavior can make you come off as emotionally needy and dependent. Whatever someone else does for you will never be enough because you'll always want more from that person: more time, more love, more concern, more of everything. Your partner can sense this and will be afraid of being consumed by your never-ending demands for attention and care. The more this happens, the less likely your partner is to want to stay in the relationship.

It's too heavy of a burden to feel totally responsible for another person's happiness. Most people want to run the other way when faced with that. A partner who tries to be everything to the other person will eventually feel resentment and anger at being put in such a demanding position. Any sense of playfulness and fun, which is so vital to an enduring relationship, will be snuffed out.

By showing respect for yourself and belief in your ability to thrive whether in a relationship or not, you'll come from a place of empowerment and strength. These attributes attract others and engender respect, making you a more desirable partner.

2. Commit to putting more fun in your life, even when you're feeling miserable.

Don't wait until your relationship is perfect to plan fun activities for yourself. Sign up for a community class to learn about kayaking, gourmet cooking, or drumming. Make a list of places in your town or a nearby one that you'd like to visit. Branch out, learn new skills, and broaden your world.

When you're active and having fun, you'll be happier. You'll also be more attractive to your partner. Individuals who are happy have a natural sex appeal that makes them desirable and draws others to them. When you're living life with gusto and a sense of adventure, regardless of the state of your relationship, your partner is more likely to want to spend time with you.

One of the biggest mistakes you can make is to wait and see what happens in your relationship before creating a more satisfying life for yourself. After all, would you rather spend time with someone who is miserable and unhappy or with someone who is doing interesting and fun things while enjoying life? Enthusiasm and a sense of fun are powerful aphrodisiacs. The more centered, balanced, and happy you are, the more you increase the odds that you'll be able to create a happy, healthy relationship.

How Do You Know You're in a Bad Relationship?

Ask yourself these questions if you think you may be in a bad relationship:

- Do you and your partner repeatedly break up and get back together?

- Have you or your partner had chronic difficulties committing to the relationship?
- Do you argue a lot?
- Have family and friends expressed concerns about your relationship?
- Do you feel the need to defend your partner to others?
- Is your partner unnecessarily suspicious of you?
- Does he or she have problems controlling his or her anger?
- Has there been an incidence of physical abuse?
- Are you concerned about your partner's alcohol or drug use?
- Do you fear for your safety?

If you answer yes to most of these questions, you are in an unhealthy relationship and it is time to make a change. This might mean addressing the issues head on, but more likely than not, it means leaving.

This may be especially difficult to do if you are married, or if there are children involved, but if you make a plan and remain committed to your decision, your safety and well-being are achievable.

Make a Commitment to Leave

The journey of a thousand miles often starts with one profound decision. Now is the time to decide that you are going to end it once and for all. The process will not be easy, and you'll need the sheer force of your conviction behind you if you are to make it through to the other end. Don't get into the trap of telling yourself, *If he or she changes this about themselves within this time frame, I will give them one more chance.* Don't do this to yourself. Make up your mind and stick with it.

Enlist Support
from Family and Friends

It is most likely that your family and friends already know that something is wrong. Perhaps they have even been on your case for ages to leave. Now is the time to let them know about your decision and how they can help. It could be that you need assistance moving or a shoulder to cry on now and then. It is important to create a safety net of family and friends before you actually leave because they are the ones who will see you through the difficult times.

Make a Clean Break

It is important that you make a clean break. The easiest way to fall back into that toxic relationship is to drag things out. Don't. It's been proven that ending relationships in small steps only prolongs the process. When children are not involved, you should not try to be friends. The future might look different, but for now, a clean break is the only way.

Let Go of the Savior Mentality

We often feel the need to rescue our partners. One of the reasons people don't get out of unhealthy relationships when they should is because they don't want to cause their partner pain. The breakup will undoubtedly cause pain for him or her, and you can't stop that from happening. It's a natural part of life and growth, so don't let that hold you back from doing what you know you have to do.

Fill the Emptiness

Once you have left your partner, you'll find that you have time on your hands that you don't know what to do with. Look at this as an opportunity to do something you've been putting off. You may want to take a class that's interested you for ages. You may get back into fitness or become more dedicated to it. You may want to begin a new hobby or spend time with friends you may have been neglecting because of the relationship. Find a way to fill the void so that you are not tempted to go back.

What If You Are Married?

Leaving a marriage can be a tremendously difficult and a brave step to take. When leaving a bad marriage, follow the same steps as if you were leaving any other romantic relationship, with the big exception of having to eventually file for a divorce.

Before you begin the process of divorce, it is important to take these additional steps:

- If you feel threatened by your partner, it is important to inform the local authorities that you are going to need help.
- Seek professional help by reaching out to support groups or counselors who are experienced in relationship issues. Also, reach out to an experienced family law attorney who will guide you through the process of divorce.
- Stop talking to your partner, especially if he or she is cunning and has used emotional blackmail to lure you back in before. This means there should be absolutely no form of communication unless you have children and need to co-parent. Where this is the case, only communicate on concerns about the children.

- File a restraining order immediately after separation if you need to, especially if you have a partner who will resort to violence to ensure that you don't leave him or her.
- Finally, file for a divorce as soon as you can. Get as far away from this person and the toxic relationship as quickly and as cleanly as possible. If there is no hope for your marriage, staying separated but not divorced will only cause more pain.

What If There Are Children Involved?

Many parents do not want to traumatize their children by separating. Often, they stay in very toxic relationships because they feel that they are protecting the kids. However, research suggests that staying together for the kids is more often than not the wrong decision. Seeing one's parents in constant conflict is more traumatic for children than seeing them split up.

It is therefore important to understand and let it sink in that while your children may experience some form of trauma from your breakup, it will not be as profound as the trauma they will experience from you staying together with a toxic partner.

My mother left my father when I was ten. I wish she had left him long before then, but she couldn't. She was a stay-at-home mom and didn't have any money to leave. She left him once before and ended up going back to him because he promised to change and go to counseling.

She went back, and they went to counseling. It eventually came out that my father agreed to go to counseling because he thought the therapist would tell my mom that she was crazy and that he was a great guy. Instead, the therapist held a mirror up to him, and he didn't like what he saw. He called the therapist a quack and refused to go back. My mom was once again stuck in an unhealthy, abusive relationship.

The first time my mom left, we went to stay with a friend of hers. The friend was supportive and would have let us stay as long as we needed to, but my mom felt like a burden. She didn't want to rely on her friend for too long. I think that's part of the reason why she went back.

Finally, the day came when she couldn't take any more. While he was at work, she told me to pack a bag with my most important belongings—only what I could carry. She called a taxi, and we went to an abused women's shelter.

The second and final time she left him, she was more prepared. She didn't have a place to stay, but she had a place to go. The women's shelter had resources in place to help. They had a room we could stay in and staff to help my mom find a job and a permanent place to live. There were bars on the windows and a security guard at the door. We were safe and supported. My mom quickly found a job and an apartment. Finally, her life could start fresh.

Planning is essential. She didn't feel bad staying at the women's shelter because its purpose was to help women like her. She didn't feel bad asking the staff for help because that was their job. There are resources available; you just have to look for them.

Whether your kids are two or twenty-two years old, do not stay on account of them. Leave *for* them. Here are tips on how to help them cope:

- *Prepare the children.* It is important that you give them an honest appraisal of how the divorce may affect their lives. The worst thing you can do is not prepare them for the outcome.

- *Make it clear* to your children that the divorce is not their fault, but rather a result of the parents' actions as adults. Let them know if the decision to leave is the last resort after unsuccessful attempts to repair the relationship. Be truthful and acknowledge your sorrow over the effect of your decision on them.

- *Children may irrationally adopt an angry stance* against you for initiating the separation, even though they can see that you are suffering in the relationship. They don't want you to continue suffering, but they likely don't want you disrupting their lives either. It is important that you acknowledge their right to be angry at how the divorce changes their world.

- As much as you can, do your best to keep things as *consistent and predictable* as possible. If you can, keep them in the same schools and do your best to keep their extracurricular schedule the same. However, this may not always be possible. When my mom left my father, we had to move to an area where she could afford an apartment. For me, that meant changing schools. At the time, I was angry and thought my life was over, and I'm sure my anger and frustration hurt her more than she let on. When I got settled into my new school, I made friends and was very happy. Kids are resilient. They may not like change, but eventually they'll be okay.

- If your partner wasn't violent, *be open to your children communicating with the other parent* and work with your ex to have consistency in parenting. If he or she was violent, however, do all you can to keep them away from the kids, especially if they are young. Do not be afraid of getting a restraining order if you have to.

Raising Self-Esteem After a Toxic Marriage: Three Strategies for Success

When a marriage ends, your self-esteem can take a nose-dive. You're making a huge life change—living arrangements, time and access to children, the quality of relationships with mutual friends and family members, and finances—and it is important to take good care of yourself during this time. Here are three strategies to boost your self-esteem after the end of a toxic marriage:

1. Make your physical health a high priority.

The mind-and-body connection is a powerful one, and supporting the health of your body can also help your emotional well-being. Eat healthy foods and avoid highly processed and sugary choices in favor of organic and unprocessed options. Take vitamins and supplements suggested by your doctor. Create a doctor-approved exercise plan; cardiovascular exercise is ideal. This will improve self-image and fitness, and it will also increase the feel-good endorphins that contribute to a sense of well-being.

2. Spend time around people who love and support you.

Friends and family can be very helpful in offering emotional support and filling your time. You need to hear positive, affirming messages about who you are and your capability and worth. Also, it may be beneficial to seek out a counselor, as he or she can offer a trained, unbiased perspective and help you process your emotions surrounding the marriage and divorce. When you are ready to start moving forward and setting new goals for yourself, a life coach is another advocate and accountability partner to help get you where you want to go.

3. Avoid interacting with your ex, especially in the beginning.

You need time to heal, away from the toxic source. It is likely your ex will continue trying to employ the same techniques to control you or engage in the same hurtful behaviors that ended your marriage. Give yourself time to gain perspective and become stronger in yourself. If you must interact due to children, limit conversations to that topic and disengage if the conversation becomes personal or off topic.

Ending a romance is never easy. When you enter into a relationship, you want nothing more than for it to work out and hope this is your forever. I have seen many people struggling in their relationships and trying all that they can to make it work. When both partners are still committed to each other and see a future together, I encourage them to do their best to save their relationship. But let's face it, not all relationships are salvageable, and you should never stay in a toxic relationship just for the sake of attachment.

Assessing the Relationship

Relationships take work. You can't just leave a relationship to its own devices and hope that things will improve miraculously. How can a bumpy relationship improve without putting in the effort to make it work?

I want you to try this exercise:

1. Write down on a piece of paper a list of reasons that made you fall in love with your partner.

2. List the things your partner does that make you happy, that let you know he or she still loves you.

3. Now, write down what it is about the relationship that you feel has changed. How would you like to see the relationship improve moving forward?

4. List a few concrete examples of things that have upset you. Oftentimes your other half may not even realize he or she has upset you. If you don't communicate, then your partner will never know and therefore will not be able to amend the behavior.

5. Using the list from number four, give examples of how you wished your partner had handled a bothersome situation differently. This is important to help him or her know what you need. Don't expect your partner to be a mind reader. Be specific. This will help the next time something similar happens.

6. Moving forward, how would you like to see your relationship with this person change? What do you need from that person?

Writing your feelings on paper can really help to solidify your understanding of the situation and what you would like to see changed. Certain things can remain hidden in our minds but articulating those feelings and committing them to paper allows you to access them more clearly.

7. Now, this is the hardest part of this exercise. I want you to tell your partner how you feel and how you would like your relationship to change. You can either do this in-person or through an email.

Some people find it easier to get things out in writing than face-to-face. Try to use "I feel" language versus "you did this" and make sure to reinforce that you are having this conversation because you love your partner and want the relationship to be better. Be prepared for your partner to become defensive and feel personally attacked. This is a natural human reaction. If you see this start to happen, pause the conversation and come back to it another time when he or she has had time to think about things.

8.   Give your partner time to digest what you've asked. Try starting the conversation by asking him or her to take some time to think about what you are bringing up. Try not to get defensive and angry. If the conversation seems to be going off the rails, then step away and try again when that person has had time to ruminate on what you are asking.

9.   Ask your partner if there are any changes he or she would like to see in the relationship. If you are unhappy, there is a good chance your partner is too. Be open to hearing their needs and accepting that there may be things you need to change in the relationship too.

10. Finally, put a time limit on seeing changes happen. Change will not happen overnight. You need to give it time and offer patience and support to help make things improve for both of you. However, it is completely reasonable to put a time limit on your partner altering his or her behavior toward you in a positive way. You don't need to stay in an unhealthy or unhappy relationship for too long. It is reasonable to move on if your existing relationship isn't fulfilling you the way it once was, especially after putting in effort to make it better.

CHAPTER SEVEN

Toxic Friendships

Letting go of toxic people in your life
is a big step in loving yourself.

—Hussein Nishah

F riendships can be as equally challenging to end as romantic relationships since, historically, we don't "break up"
with friends in any sort of formal way.

A lot of times, we stay in toxic friendships because we feel
bad, we don't want to be lonely, or we don't know how to end
the friendship. We might hope they will change, but more often
than not, they won't.

Learn to recognize a toxic friendship and demand more for
yourself. If your friend isn't willing to give you what you need,
then it's healthiest to end the relationship.

Here are the signs to look for:

- The friend tries to control you, directly or through manipulation.
- He or she disregards your boundaries and seems to thrive on violat-
  ing and disrespecting any boundaries you set.

- These friends never admit to being wrong. They're always right and will find ways to prove it.
- They often play the victim and will blame their career, relationship problems, or anything else on others. Oftentimes, this includes you.
- A toxic friend loves to take from you without giving anything back, whether it is your money, your clothes, or your time.
- They guilt-trip and manipulate you into feeling like you're a bad person because you're not spending enough time with them or responding immediately to their requests.

Many of us have experienced toxic friendships at one point in our lives. They leave us feeling angry, frustrated, irritated, confused, miserable, and drained, and yet, you can't seem to say no to the person.

Some time ago, I woke up to the fact that a friend of mine, I'll call her Samantha, was irritating me profoundly. The cause of our friction was a fundamental personality difference: I am usually positive and optimistic, while Samantha was negative and constantly complained about everything in her life. I became ever more sensitive to her whining and, in turn, complained about her to other friends. I spent more and more time being irritated, then frustrated, and then downright angry at Samantha, and it drained me.

We've probably all felt trapped in a toxic relationship from time to time. If we're lucky, the toxic situation is short-lived or resolves itself, and we can move on with no hurt feelings. Sometimes, though, the toxicity takes hold and just drags on, draining our energy and happiness. It can be damaging to stay in a negative frame of mind for too long dealing with the bad stuff, which steals what we need for the good things in our lives.

The Toxic Friend and Self-Improvement

When we start to make positive changes and improve our-selves, we expect friends to be excited and happy for us. Nobody wants a close friendship to turn toxic. I can tell you firsthand how it's devastating when formerly close friendships crash and burn during a time that should be exciting for you. A toxic friendship doesn't always mean that your best friend is actively sabotaging you *Mean Girls* style. It can happen if you've chosen different paths and grown apart.

If you are transforming your life with positive changes, whether it's gaining confidence in yourself, losing weight, or starting a new career, it's almost certain you're going to lose friends. People who aren't comfortable with change will find your evolving life hard to deal with, maybe because it reminds them of their own stagnant life or they aren't used to you stand-ing up for yourself. Maybe your whole friendship was based on the negative behaviors that you have left behind.

Self-improvement will expose the friends who don't have your best interests at heart. Be prepared to lose friends. It will hurt a lot, and then you'll get over it and find happiness. It can be a blessing in disguise.

The thing about toxic friends is that sometimes they don't mean to be horrible. People are terrified of change and can't understand new perspectives. Most toxic friends will talk behind your back or be judgmental of your goals; they leave you feeling drained, negative, or down about yourself every time you see them. They aren't bad people, but that doesn't change the fact they're bad for your personal growth.

Take a good look at your friendships and notice who is trying to pull you back into your bad habits, who cuts you off
when you're sharing something you're proud of, who tells you
that you're not a good friend because you're not giving them all
of your attention. Those are the kind of people you don't need.

I look back at my former group of friends with love and
respect for the time we spent together, but at the same time,
I know they were toxic to my improved self. I don't gossip or
enjoy having shallow conversations all the time, but I did with
them. I chose to be positive and work toward the future instead
of being stuck in the past. Unfortunately, that caused awkward-
ness and distance in the friendships. People grow apart and
choose different paths; mine didn't have room for their negative energy.

I'm not encouraging you to cut off friends who don't agree
with you all the time or have different goals than you. I'm
encouraging you to recognize the friends who are authentic and
supportive—proud of your achievements rather than expressing jealousy—and surround yourself with them.

Ending a friendship doesn't have to be a big, dramatic fight.
If you want to save the friendship, you can try discussing your
feelings. Maybe they don't realize how they're affecting you
and can shift their attitude. If that's not the case, you have two
options: you can directly say you need some space, or slowly
stop spending time with them. Leaving it on a good note leaves
room for reconnection if you feel they may grow in the future.

Here's the hard part. Even if these friends don't mean to be
toxic and are generally good people, they are what they are and
you have to move on. Leaving a friendship is just as hard as

leaving a romantic relationship, especially if you still love and respect that friend.

I had one particular friend when we were teenagers, and our friendship remained strong through our youth. In our twenties, things changed in both our lives. My friend started to resent me for the path I had taken, acting passive-aggressively all the time. She was not happy with the choices I was making that were different from hers. I was happy for her, but she did not reciprocate that happiness.

Before I decided to "break up" with her, I spent a good year feeling bad about myself and guilty when I wasn't with her. So much of my time was consumed with her feelings about me and my life choices that it stopped me from being happy and living the life I wanted.

I knew I had to remove myself from the relationship, but it was hard. I didn't want to hurt her, but our friendship was hurting me. I finally decided I loved myself enough to put *me* first. We often think that we are supposed to be selfless and only think of others first. That is not necessarily the best advice. You are not being selfish if you take care of yourself first. You don't have to intentionally hurt others, but you also don't have to be in a situation where other people's happiness means yours is extinguished.

You are not responsible for others' happiness. Be kind, compassionate, and caring to others as long as you are being kind, caring, and compassionate to yourself as well.

Just because people aren't happy about your amazing progress doesn't mean you should hide it. Toxic friends have their own underlying issues that cause them to act in unsupportive ways; don't take it personally. It's an indicator they aren't happy with themselves or their lives. You worked hard to manifest change in your life, so don't let a few doubters dull your success. Surround yourself with awesome friends who are proud of you and push you to do better. Any friend who doesn't leave you feeling uplifted, supported, and happy isn't a true a friend. Life is too short to associate with people who don't appreciate the beautiful soul that you are. Just know that you are not the only person to go through this. It may feel lonely now, but soon you'll find people who will appreciate who you are and who you are trying to be, and it won't feel forced or lonely.

Follow your intuition. If someone is constantly bringing you down, it may be time to reconsider the friendship.

A case study of two friends: Marie is thirty-six years old, single, loud, and a heavy drinker who talks obsessively about how men are all jerks. Amber is thirty-two, happily married, and has a baby on the way. Marie started a restaurant blog, and one month later began boasting to anyone who would listen that she already had more than 300 comments on her blog. Amber was one of the first to comment and is very supportive of Marie. At the same time, Amber began a mental health blog and wondered why she wasn't getting any comments. "Will you comment on my blog?" she asked Marie, hoping to at least get one.

A week passed and Marie had still not commented. Amber asked why, to which Marie looked away and replied, "I'm sorry, I'm almost never on my computer."

"Then how did you get 300 people interested in your blog?" Amber asked.

"I don't know, I guess people just really want to read about good food."

Amber was naturally put out that Marie wouldn't even make one comment for her, especially because she was an early supporter of her friend. Amber began to wonder whether Marie might be withholding something.

With no marketing knowledge, Amber banged her head against a wall night after night as she tried to understand how to get her blog noticed. Sure, she received the odd comment, but nowhere near Marie's activity.

A few weeks later at a party, Amber bumped into a very drunk Marie and her friend Jessica, the archetypal tech genius who lived, breathed, and dreamed computers. She spoke of programming and coding and things that neither Amber nor Marie understood. And then she revealed the truth. "I've been helping Marie with her blog, and I'd love to help you, too," she said to Amber.

"That's so kind of you," Amber replied. "Tell me, how exactly did you help Marie?"

"Well, I designed her blog page and I used SEO and other tools. Now she has more than 5,000 followers."

Marie had been taking all the credit for someone else's work, and she had been unwilling to share the information to help her friend. But why?

"Jessica's going to help me with my blog," Amber said when Marie returned from getting more drinks, but Marie said nothing and sulked the rest of the night.

A few days later, Jessica called Amber. "I'll help you, but you must keep it to yourself. Marie is adamant that I shouldn't."

"But why?" said Amber. "Our blogs aren't even remotely related or competing with one another."

"I don't get it either," said Jessica. "I think she's just really insecure."

Amber suddenly understood what sort of person Marie was. She stopped returning Marie's calls, ignored her emails, and essentially walked away. Was that really Amber's only option? Could she have confronted Marie and given her a chance to apologize? What would you do in Amber's situation?

How to Get Back in Control

Get a bigger-picture view by finding a moment to be alone in a safe, supportive location, and take some deep breaths to relax. Close your eyes and visualize your current relationship. What do you notice? How are you behaving? Do you like what you see? What would someone else notice about the situation? In the case of Samantha and me, I was shocked when I realized I was going behind her back and complaining to others, something I am still not proud of. I didn't like this picture of myself, and it was eye-opening to see it.

How much of your time and energy are you spending dealing with or responding to the person or situation? When I was most angry and frustrated with Samantha, I spent up to two hours a day (at least ten hours a week) either dealing with her, complaining about her, or just being angry.

If you don't like the image of yourself, answer these important questions below. It can be helpful to write your answers on a piece of paper. Getting them out of your head and seeing them written down can help solidify your true feelings surrounding the relationship:

- Is it worth it to stay in this situation or relationship? (The answer might be "yes," especially if it is limited in time.)
- What is best for me?
- What are my goals or purpose for this relationship or situation, and are they being met?
- What else could I do with that time and energy spent on this person?
- If I met this person today, would I like him or her?
- What am I tolerating that isn't serving me?
- Do I want the friendship to improve or end? What steps will I take to make this happen?

Ways of Dealing with a Toxic Friend

People can be insecure and sometimes it's impossible to be happy for someone else's successes if they are miserable in their own lives. This is particularly understandable if your success hits them exactly where they are insecure. However, when they actively try to harm, sabotage, or boycott your success, that's too far. Worse even is when the friend's goals aren't even remotely related to yours, yet he or she still can't bear to watch you succeed.

When a friend has been selfish and deceitful to the point that this person wishes you ill, you can deal with it in one of the following ways:

Confront them. Be prepared for the possibility that instead of bowing their head in shame and apologizing, the person might try to justify the action, turn it around, and even make it look like you are in the wrong. *Attempt this approach ONLY if you are certain of your argument.* Pick one message that you wish to convey. In Amber's case, she could repeat, "Did you or did you not tell me that you didn't know how you got so many comments on your blog?" Do not allow yourself to be sidetracked with other arguments or led down paths where the person lists things that you did wrong in the past. No one is perfect. You've probably made mistakes too at some point in your friendship, but for the purposes of our argument, that is not the point. Don't allow the other person to deflect just so that they can win the argument.

Try to help them. Again, beware, for in order to accept your help, the other person must first be willing to accept that they have behaved wrongly. If Amber approached Marie and said, "I know you tried to sabotage my endeavors, but I value our friendship enough that I'd like to help you," Marie might deny it outright and turn it against Amber.

Forgive and forget. Unless you have the discipline of a shaman who sleeps on a bed of nails every night, this option rarely works. It especially depends on the severity of the actions. You may tell yourself it wasn't all that bad, but it will eat into your trust of that person. It is likely that you will no longer view that friend with the same love, respect, and regard as you did previously. Eventually, resentment will build up. I recommend against this option unless you have the self-discipline to *truly* forgive and forget.

Walk away. Sadly, unless your friend is the type of person whose vocabulary includes, "I'm sorry, I messed up, please forgive me," walking away is often the only option you have. Most toxic people are not familiar with asking for forgiveness, which is why most of their victims choose to walk away without a word.

Find a reason within yourself to end the situation or relationship. When you break a relationship for self-preservation, you will find an inner strength instead of punishing or otherwise getting back at others. When it's about you, no one has grounds to attack you, manipulate you, or guilt-trip you into remaining in the toxic mess. Alternately, if you have to remain in the mess for a while (say, a team project at work that's in meltdown but has a deadline and will end), getting centered can help you gain clarity and hold some inner peace during the process.

Focus on the how, not the why. Instead of pointing fingers, blaming and shaming, having a significant showdown, or lashing out in retaliation, focus on your own behavior and what it will take to get clear of this relationship and the negativity it brings to your life. If you are dialed in to your own personal reasons for leaving, then the way out will become clear.

It's never easy to leave, no matter what, and you have to be strong. If the situation demands defusing, disentanglement, or an unavoidable confrontation, be prepared. Keep that big-picture view, focus on your personal reasons, and stick to your plans. When communicating with others, keep your comments focused on yourself. Yes, it may hurt the person when you break away, but their happiness is not your responsibility.

It is okay to walk away from a toxic friendship. Your friend may be having a hard time, and you're afraid that leaving will create more hardship, but that's not on you. Your responsibility is for yourself and your mental well-being.

CHAPTER EIGHT

Stop Comparing Your Life to Others'

> When you are content to be simply
> yourself and don't compare or compete,
> everybody will respect you.
>
> —Lao Tzu

It should come as no shock that comparing yourself to others is one of the worst things you can do for your self-esteem. If you are constantly comparing, then you'll never be happy. If you're too worried about what everyone else is doing, then you aren't putting the energy into your life that you should. Perhaps one of the reasons you've not attained real happiness or that you don't feel successful is because you are measuring yourself with another person's yardstick.

By comparing yourself to others, you are making assumptions about them. These are almost always wrong. By envying others, you are damaging your mental health based on something that might not even be true. Comparing ourselves with other people allows them to drive our behavior, whether they are aware of it or not. This is too much power to give to someone else.

When I started my business, I had a competitor who was always watching what I did. I created a Facebook group, and she invited each person who joined my group to join hers also. I made a YouTube video promoting my Facebook page, and then she made an identical video. Everything she did was a reaction to what I did. Rather than focusing on her own business and the happiness she wanted from it, she was consumed with what I was doing.

I can't imagine any of this was fun for her. Yes, you should keep tabs on your competitors, but to mimic them all the time isn't healthy. Ultimately, she sold her business and it fizzled out. Things might have turned out differently for her if she had just focused on her uniqueness and what she had to offer.

We often envy others when they are better at something than we are. We compare ourselves to Mary, who does better PowerPoint presentations, and to Bob, who seems to have a more exciting love life than we do, and to Mike, whose children seem much better behaved than ours. Comparison, when accurate, can be motivating. However, it's more often than not inaccurate and destructive.

In a world that demands perfection, people are constantly comparing and competing with one another to stay ahead. When we do this, we often end up slowing down our own efforts of improvement. If my competitor wasn't so concerned with what I was doing, she could have focused on her own goals and interests in order to flourish instead of fail.

If you are constantly comparing yourself to others, you're wasting time and energy in looking at what you don't have rather than focusing on what you do have and striving for what you *want*. Find contentment in your life—love who you are and put effort into changes you want to make.

I have always struggled with my opinion of myself and my circumstances. I grew up poor, so everyone always seemed to have more than I did. I resented everyone. I was miserable most of the time because of it. As I grew into adulthood and developed the ability to be more self-reflective, I realized how much I was comparing myself to others and the harm it was causing me.

I didn't know who I was or what I wanted in life. I knew who I wasn't and what I didn't have. That's a big difference.

I had to stop and take an active look at how I perceived myself and my life. I remember being maybe five years old and jealous of my neighbor, whose parents gave her whatever she wanted. She had a million Barbie dolls and I had one fake Barbie that was made of cheap plastic. Its legs didn't even bend. At the time, this summed up my life; it was made of cheap plastic. If I wanted to be happy, I had to stop comparing myself and my life to others.

The Pitfalls of Comparison

Do you base your happiness on how you stack up against a neighbor, a coworker, a sibling, a friend, or a family member? It is easy to think that if you had her body, her house, her knowledge, her husband, her job, her beauty, her intelligence, her personality, or her money, you'd be happy. That kind of thinking is a trap. When we compare ourselves with others, we presuppose there is one right way to *be*. There isn't. Everyone has good qualities. Everyone has great worth. And everyone is unique.

If all of our worth is focused outside of us, our self-esteem will rise and fall as external circumstances change. If we struggle with illness or aging and someone younger, richer, prettier, or smarter moves in next door, suddenly we feel worthless. That's a miserable way to live.

The truth is there will always be someone who is better than we are in almost every area of life, just as there will always be someone who isn't at our own level. We can't compare ourselves with others without becoming either arrogant or insecure.

You started life with a personalized package of gifts and challenges. No one else has lived your life, so no one else can be compared with you.

Good Comparisons

If you occasionally compare yourself to others, it can be a good thing. As long as you don't connect such comparisons with self-worth, you can become inspired to reach further and achieve more. This type of positive self-comparison motivates and drives your ambition. Don't let comparison between you and others become a detriment to your mental health and self-image by only focusing on what they have and you don't.

Stopping the destructive side of the comparison game is not hard. The more often you practice, the easier it gets.

Step 1: Become aware of self-comparison. This is an important step. As I said earlier, some self-comparisons can be useful, but most of the time, they are not.

Step 2: Isolate good comparisons from bad. Exchange envy for admiration. Set a reasonable goal for yourself that uses this good comparison to motivate you.

Step 3: Celebrate your uniqueness. Your value as a person has little to do with what you look like or possess. When you compare yourself to someone else, you deny your own wonderful gifts and talents. Everyone has worth, but the source of that worth is as different as each individual.

Step 4: Compare yourself to yourself. I am always striving to do something better than I did before. I take the lessons and combine them with qualities I admire in others to strive for a new personal best. I use my past successes and failures as my yardstick to be in competition with myself and no one else.

Always compare yourself with yourself first. When you compare yourself with others, start by *admiring* their achievements and strengths. Think in terms of awe, inspiration, motivation, and respect. Feelings like jealousy, hatred, resentfulness, rivalry, and spite feed negativity and depression. Let go of such inner darkness, and you will have room to embrace the light.

Habits That Lower Self-Esteem and Lead to Depression

When our self-esteem is low, we're at higher risk for depression. Self-esteem includes positive and negative self-evaluations. Good self-esteem reflects self-respect and implies a feeling of worth that's not determined by comparison to, or approval from, others. Self-acceptance is even more profound. It's a feeling of being good enough, neither perfect nor inadequate. We feel we have worth and deserve love, not merely because of beauty, talent, achievement, intelligence, status, or popularity. It's a sense of inner contentment.

Positive self-esteem is essential for enjoying life and experiencing healthy relationships that endure. The following bad habits can make you feel insecure, ashamed, anxious, sad, and hopeless:

- Negatively comparing yourself to others
- Finding fault with yourself
- Tyrannizing yourself with *should haves*
- Projecting self-criticism onto others and imagining they're judging you
- Not trying new things to avoid failing
- Procrastinating
- Doubting your instincts and decisions
- Ignoring your needs and wants
- Not setting boundaries and allowing abuse, criticism, or exploitation
- Refusing to forgive yourself

When we compare ourselves to someone else, whether favorably or unfavorably, we measure ourselves by an external standard. Feeling "better than" someone is really a means to compensate for underlying shame and low self-esteem.

It would be helpful to evaluate why we need to compare ourselves to someone else. When we compare ourselves negatively, we feel inferior, lose confidence, and like ourselves less. It depresses our mood and discourages us.

An active *inner critic* has us constantly thinking about what we should and should not do and makes us second-guess what we've already done. Habitual faultfinding can cause us to assume others see us as we see ourselves. In this way, we project our critic onto others and then anticipate and feel the effects of criticism or judgment that we imagine, even when none occurs.

Lowered self-confidence causes us to fear making mistakes, looking foolish, or failing. Our self-esteem is always on the line, so it's safer not to try anything new to avoid appearing incompetent. This is another reason we procrastinate in tackling tasks or experiences that are new or challenging. At the same time, we nag and criticize ourselves for failing to accomplish our goals. Rather than take a chance, we make ourselves out to be wrong for not trying, which ensures failure and low self-esteem.

Caring what others think about us from an early age leaves us unsure of our values and beliefs. It encourages reliance on others. When we are too concerned with how others will react to us and the decisions we make, then we put others' opinions before our needs and wants. Decision-making becomes difficult, even paralyzing. Low self-esteem and shame heighten our fear of making mistakes, leading to self-doubt, insecurity, and indecision. Instead, we avoid action or look to others for validation, opinions, and answers, which further undermines our self-trust and self-esteem.

Accommodating others alienates us from our needs and wants. By not acknowledging, expressing, and meeting our needs and wants, we're admitting to ourselves and others that they're not important; ergo, we're not important. Taking responsibility to meet our needs and/or ask for them (such as seeking out a raise at work) builds self-esteem. When we don't, we feel like helpless victims of circumstance.

Not feeling worthy of love and respect, denied to us by ourselves, makes us vulnerable to abuse and exploitation. We excuse or rationalize being abused or disrespected. Dependent upon others' approval, we're afraid to set boundaries lest we alienate those we love or need. We're quick to blame ourselves and readily accept blame from others because we're guilt-ridden due to shame. Although we forgive the mistakes of others, especially if we receive an apology, we're not as kind to ourselves. In fact, we can punish or hold a grudge against ourselves for years over past mistakes.

Five Tips to Improve Self-Esteem

Low self-esteem is a powerful manipulator that can control us for a long time if we let it. Have you wished to be able to flip a switch and change your attitude and mood? Has someone ever hurt your feelings, and their words made you feel insecure about who you are? If you answered "yes" to any of these questions, follow these hints to help boost your self-esteem.

1. *Appreciate yourself.* Be thankful for your gifts and talents. There are many gifts you have that others do not, and it's time to appreciate them. For example, remind yourself that "I am a great reader," "I am a great listener," "I am a great helper," and so on.

2. *Avoid being judgmental toward others.* At times, people are notorious for gossiping and talking about others. Stop this habit if you find yourself participating. It shows insecurity about yourself, and it only makes you feel worse afterward.

3. *Don't compare yourself to anyone else.* Comparing only makes you think of everything you don't have and causes your self-esteem to

drop. You're a unique person, so just be you and learn to accept the person you are.

4. *Make a few goals that you can reach and work toward them.* Set goals for yourself, like asking for a raise or applying for a new job. Also set smaller goals, like not watching television until the weekend, for a validating feeling of accomplishment. Aim for goals that will help you accomplish things you want to get done. Achieving goals, even small ones, is a big booster for self-esteem.

5. *Make a contribution.* Do something to help others, and you will feel great. For example, help a friend with their résumé, offer to take your elderly neighbor shopping, volunteer for something, and so forth. It is helpful for everyone involved.

Believe me when I say that you have high value with a unique set of abilities. If you don't know your potential, it's time to find out. Judging yourself against someone else is not the way to do this. Their success or failure does not determine your value. You do.

You are capable of so much more when you stop looking at your shortcomings and failures. The real question is what you are going to do with your potential. Your purpose reaches far wider than the little space so many of us find ourselves in. Your unique abilities are meant to make a difference in this world. This is true for every person, including you! Deep down, you know if you are living up to this potential.

Your dreams are not too big or unrealistic. Be honest with yourself. When you *believe* you can do something, the answer to *how* will come when you open up to the possibility. You are the one who has the ultimate power in deciding your own value.

When you see your value, you won't need to compare yourself to others. All you need to do is endeavor to reach your own potential.

So, what do you do if you catch yourself comparing? Change your focus. If the other person is succeeding with their talents and abilities, that's great. Allow that to inspire you to succeed at your own goals. If they are struggling and falling short of their greatness, why would you want to see that as a reflection on you? Honor their journey as separate from yours. You will be far more productive, focusing on fulfilling your own potential rather than how you compare to others.

From now on, let go of this old habit of self-sabotage. It doesn't serve you well and may discourage you from being all you can be.

Acceptance

Well-meaning people may tell you that you have no right to feel sorry for yourself and should put a smile on your face. If you would simply change your attitude, you would be doing better than you are.

Ignore those well-meaning people. Your feelings are yours. Don't let others attempt to manipulate your emotions. It helps to be optimistic when you can. Often, this requires a process. You may feel sad or angry at first. Even when you have processed your immediate issues, there will be more issues to sort through and you may have more bad days.

Denying your situation keeps you from accepting it. When you accept your pain, you can be free from its chains. Do you accept your life as it is now? If not, can you identify what is blocking your acceptance?

I knew someone who refused to accept the reality of her life and for months used to admit she was hitting her head against a wall. When I saw her last, she was smiling and told me she had finally accepted her life. She said, "The only good thing about hitting your head against the wall is that it feels so good to stop."

Do you know if you are hitting your head against the wall? What will happen if you stop?

Practicing acceptance means that you accept yourself, others, and circumstances just as they are. Take responsibility for things you have control over and surrender the rest. Practice acceptance by telling yourself what you are working on accepting and have already accepted. If someone tells you they don't accept you or something about you, it's their issue and not yours.

You don't have to defend yourself when you are being questioned. If it's a self-care decision, saying you feel it is appropriate is enough. If you don't want to meet a friend for a drink because you're not feeling social, it's okay to say, "No, thank you." You don't have to explain yourself to anyone. Some people will try to guilt you into making a decision that is contrary to what you need. When you accept yourself and decide to take care of your needs, that's when you'll start to feel happier and healthier. Practice saying no without explanation, and be confident that you are doing what is right for you.

Just Be Yourself

How many times do you hear the advice *just be yourself* uttered as if it's a magical solution to all social woes? What do I need to do to fit in? *Just be yourself*. But how can you be yourself if you are too busy focusing on how others perceive you or how you believe you compare to others? It's hard to be yourself if you are consumed by wanting to be someone else.

Start with being genuine. To be genuine is to do the things you believe in and want to be accepted for. There's no value in pretending to be something you are not. Don't worry about what other people might think. Respect the opinions of others, but don't let them push you in a different direction if you don't agree. Don't compare yourself to other people. When you do, you risk losing your own identity because you become focused on what someone else has that you don't. There is no need to compete with or outshine others. It won't make you better. Being humble and content with who you are and the opinions you have can go a long way to increasing your self-esteem. Acceptance comes more freely when you're happy to acknowledge your weaknesses as well as strengths.

Maintain a positive self-image. Why is this important? Good self-esteem is necessary to maintain a good impression of yourself, your life, and the world around you. Those who suffer from low self-esteem may also suffer from depression and low self-worth. They constantly rely on the praise of others to give their lives meaning and value. Maintaining self-esteem is vital for you to enjoy life to its fullest, to assist you in being successful and productive, and to help you feel good about yourself.

Low self-esteem does not discriminate. It can affect anyone and everyone. Lots of men and women silently nurse feelings of inferiority in so many different areas of their lives. Sometimes, the origin of low self-worth cannot be easily traced to an obvious source. In many instances, feelings of inferiority can also be connected to childhood trauma.

Whatever the reason, it's essential for everyone to truly conquer this problem. Overcoming low self-esteem is not an easy, overnight task. An individual, sometimes with the help of a professional, must determine the sources of his or her negative thoughts and take systematic steps toward overcoming the emotional problems and improving one's self.

A giant step toward overcoming low self-esteem is to stop comparing yourself to others. This tendency often begins during childhood. Children who are always compared to other siblings usually end up with a considerable amount of emotional insecurities, which are often carried to adulthood and become an integral part of an individual's personality.

If you suffer from this kind of emotional pain, take an honest look at yourself. Do you compare yourself with others too much? Do you habitually criticize yourself for no good reason? You must realize that you have innate positive qualities that cannot be compared to anyone else. You must also recognize that all people are not created perfectly. It is true that you have flaws. Everyone does, even the greatest men and women who ever lived. So, instead of focusing on your shortcomings, identify your strengths and capitalize on your positive qualities. By being kind and true to yourself, you will be well on the way toward overcoming your low self-esteem and becoming a much better person.

For a very long time, I was extremely jealous of one family member. She had what seemed like the ideal life: a husband, two kids, a house, two cars, a cottage, and more. I'd go to her house, see all that she had, and become very depressed. She didn't need to work because her husband made enough money so she could stay at home with her kids. To me, she was living the ideal life of luxury.

I felt sad and envious that I didn't have what she had. I resented being around her because in my eyes, she flaunted it. I couldn't give my kids what her kids had, and it made me feel like my life wasn't as good as hers.

Then one day, her world blew up. The husband left her, and she went from having everything to nothing. I look at her life now and wouldn't wish what happened to her on anyone. Needless to say, I am no longer jealous or envious of her. I look back at those years of envy as wasted energy. I should not have looked at her life and felt like mine was less because I didn't have all that she did. Instead, I should have worked at getting to a place where I was content with what I had.

I have a husband who loves me unconditionally, supports me no matter what, and makes me a better person because he is my rock. I have two healthy children who love each other and enjoy a great relationship. I have a job I love because I spent years educating and improving myself to get the things in life that I wanted.

Don't waste time and energy resenting what you don't have. Instead, spend the time and energy working toward what you want to get out of life and propelling your life forward. We become stagnant in life due to our envy of others. There is nothing wrong with wanting more out of life, with wanting what others have. Let that *want* turn into motivation and positive energy rather than *envy*.

Three keys to maintaining healthy self-esteem are to stop your inner critic, practice the art of self-nurturing, and seek help from others. We all have thoughts that tell us we have failed or we are not as good as others. The key to healthy self-esteem is knowing how to combat those feelings and realize they are only passing negative thoughts brought forward by inner doubt. They are not true.

Self-nurturing is a wonderful way to boost self-esteem and take care of your emotional needs. It helps you to lead a better, healthier life that is full of love and appreciation of yourself. Make sure you're getting enough sleep, eating healthy, treating yourself, and rewarding your accomplishments. Plan relaxation time and forgive yourself when you make a mistake.

Seeking the help of others is needed for those who are not good at maintaining self-esteem on their own. A professional counselor or a support group can help you to express your feelings and get to the bottom of why your self-esteem is so low.

Maintain positive self-esteem daily. There are several things that you can do each day to not only maintain your current level of self-esteem, but also gain new admiration for yourself.

- *Repeat Affirmations*—speak positive statements about yourself and your strengths out loud, which can be used to boost your confidence at a time when you need it most.
- *Don't Compare Yourself with Others*—I've said this a lot, but that's just how important it is. No one has the same situations in life, and it just isn't feasible for you to compare yourself with anyone else. You can only do your best and should never try to do someone else's best.
- *Set Goals*—Always set goals for what you want to accomplish each day, month, or year, and then reward yourself each time you reach

those goals. They don't have to be big goals. Small steps toward attainable goals will always lead you to a better self-image.

- *Release Negative Feelings*—Learn how to let go of bad feelings about yourself. Find ways to boost your confidence instead of tearing it down. Say, every day, *I like me.*

Maintaining good self-esteem is crucial to living a happy and healthy life. The stress and anxiety that comes from poor self-esteem can be damaging to you, both mentally and emotionally. Using these tips and steps, you'll build a positive self-image, boost your self-confidence, maintain your self-esteem, and live a better, happier life.

Imposter Syndrome

The reason most of us feel such a compelling need to compare ourselves to others is due to a little monster called imposter syndrome. This is a crushing belief that you are not deserving of the success that you have. It convinces you that you're not *quite* as talented, creative, intelligent, or interesting as you seem.

Deep down inside, you suspect that you have achieved success by a stroke of good fortune. Deeper still is the fear that you will one day be uncovered as a fraud who doesn't deserve the happiness in your life.

If you suffer from imposter syndrome, you're carrying around very negative thoughts about yourself. These may look like:

- I can't do this job well.
- Other people are better than me.
- My opinion is worth less than others'.

- Other people find things easier than I do.
- Other people are more confident than I am.
- Other people are more secure than I am.
- People don't let things bother them as much as I do.
- I'm not the sort of person to be really successful.
- I'm only fooling people into thinking I can do this.

Imposter syndrome is often linked to other manifestations of self-doubt, such as self-sabotage, fear of failure, or fear of success. You worry that you will be exposed, rejected, and isolated. Perhaps you are taking on a new job, have just been promoted, started your own business, or have become a parent for the first time, and you are struck by this all-encompassing feeling that you are a lie.

Some symptoms of imposter syndrome are:

- Constant feelings of inadequacy and self-doubt
- A tendency toward perfectionism
- A fear of judgment and discovery
- A tendency to downplay your achievements

Meanwhile, all around you, every other person seems to be doing well and occupying their own positions of success so effortlessly. You arrive at this conclusion without ever knowing the inner turmoil these people to whom you are comparing yourself also go through. The only way to stop feeling like an impostor is to stop thinking like an impostor.

How to Break Free

First, realize what you are doing. Do any of the feelings I've listed seem familiar? If so, then at least they are out in the open. Recognizing and acknowledging the emotions you feel as an imposter is the first step toward ridding them from your life.

The next thing is to accept that these are just thoughts, not facts. They're only notions you have. A lot of our negative thoughts stem from childhood when someone told us we were no good at something. That does not define who you are now. If we recognize the way we are thinking, then we can change that negative thought.

Take one negative thought, write it down, and ask yourself:

- Do I really believe this?
- Can I absolutely say that it's true?
- Could I be wrong about it?
- What evidence do I have for this thought?
- How does thinking this make me feel?
- How would I feel if I didn't have this thought?
- How would I act differently?

Sitting down and being mindful of your negative thoughts will help you to see that some of these beliefs don't stand up to close scrutiny. Go further and write down some positive beliefs or thoughts:

- I am competent and good at this job.
- I can learn and develop new skills whenever I need to.
- I have achieved a lot and can achieve even more.
- My opinion is worth as much as anyone else's.

Ask yourself whether these new beliefs could be just as true as the old ones. Find evidence that supports them, act on them, and strengthen them as you did with the old beliefs.

Try to catch yourself thinking about the old thoughts and stop them in their tracks. This will take work; it won't come naturally at first, but this is part of being mindful. To be mindful is to stop and think about what is on your mind and how those thoughts make you feel. You might have what appears to be a meaningless, fleeting thought, but then all of a sudden you feel down, discouraged, or even depressed. You won't figure out why you are feeling sad until you stop and think about it.

For example, maybe you're down because you found out someone at work got a raise and you didn't. It was a fleeting thought at first, and you didn't dwell on it, but it made you feel crappy. Now you're blue, but you aren't sure why. To practice mindfulness, stop and think about what made you feel this way. You may identify the fleeting thought and feel like the person's raise is a reflection on you. You didn't get a raise because you aren't worthy of a raise. The other person is better than you. You go down into the rabbit hole of self-pity. *I suck, everyone thinks I suck, I don't deserve a raise, I don't deserve a promotion, and I don't deserve to be happy.* These are all degrading thoughts. Are they even valid? Do you know for a fact that the person at work got a raise because you suck? Of course not.

Maybe they got a raise because they asked for one. Perhaps all you have to do is ask for one too. Maybe they've been there for a longer time. Maybe they started at a lower pay rate than you did, and the company is getting everyone up to a standard pay scale.

You have two choices in this situation. You can let your thoughts run wild and continue to feel crappy, or you can choose to accept that you don't know everything about the situation and move forward feeling better. *I'm going to choose to believe that the person got a raise because he or she was earning less money than I was, and the company is making sure all their employees are at a standard pay scale to be fair to everyone.* This reason feels good. *The person got a raise because I'm a crappy worker* feels bad. Pick the answer that feels good and move on. Don't let the negative thought create a reality that isn't true.

Work on replacing negative thoughts with new, more positive ones. This isn't about deluding yourself or trying to ignore reality. Your old thoughts weren't reality either.

Another thing you can do is to get feedback from people you respect. You'll probably be surprised that their view is actually more positive than your own. And, if they do point out some areas where you can improve, then you have something concrete to work on instead of just a vague idea in your head that you're somehow *not good enough*.

The following exercise was devised to uncover the shame underlying the fear of being *found out*. It takes some courage to do this exercise, but trust yourself and be brave.

1. Set a timer for three minutes and make a list of as many things as you are tolerating in your life. These are things you want to change but don't because you think you can't or don't know how.

2. Choose three things that stand out above all others. Now, choose one that you would feel embarrassed or even ashamed of if people found out.

3. Breathe. Notice your emotions surrounding the list. It is a barometer of your sense of worth at this moment. Ask yourself if you are willing to shift the way this shows up in your life. Be honest with yourself.

4. If the answer to number three is yes, make a decision right now to get the needed help to transform this aspect of your life. Write the email, make the call, do what it takes to get the support you need.

Consult a support group, mentor, coach, therapist, or wise friend, and share this with one of these trusted people. Shame cannot live in the dark. Your fear of being found out will begin to dwindle, and you will move forward a more positive, stronger version of yourself.

In this chapter, we've discussed how comparing you to others is damaging to your self-esteem. I want to encourage you to accept that you deserve every good thing in your life. You are as worthy of happiness and success as the next person. You have your own personal set of struggles, but you also have your own personal set of strengths. You deserve every good thing that comes your way.

Because you are so deserving, no one compares to you. No one can do what you're meant to do. To create this ideal life, you must take the steps toward it. You deserve to achieve your lifelong dreams, but you'll only reach those when you believe you will and actively work toward those goals.

In my experience, if we put our hearts into something, and are willing to work for it and give what it takes, it will happen. You decide if you are worthy or not. I urge you to decide to believe in yourself.

CHAPTER NINE

What If Bad Experiences Were Just Experiences?

The pessimist sees difficulty
in every opportunity.
The optimist sees opportunity
in every difficulty.

—Winston Churchill

My first question to you: Is your glass half-empty or half-full?

The objective truth is that the water is at the 50 percent point in the glass, so either description (half-full or half-empty) is true, but this question is not about technicality and right answers. This question is a matter of perception. Your perception matters a great deal.

While the objective truth is that the glass contains water at the halfway mark, the rest is up to how we interpret that truth.

For ages, the half-full, half-empty question has been used to differentiate between optimists and pessimists. An optimist is someone that sees the glass as half full, focusing on what is there rather than what is not. An optimist sees that so much can be done with half a glass of water and will look on the bright side. By nature, they are eternally hopeful and search for the good in every situation.

On the other hand, pessimists often see a glass as half-empty. He or she sees what the glass is lacking. In the mind of a pessimist, there is water missing from what could be a full glass. This type of person tends to be negative, even though they claim to be a realist.

Now, I want to paint a slightly different picture for you of a glass of water at the 50 percent point.

We all face obstacles in life. How we respond to them makes all the difference in the world. So, are you someone who sees the positive, even in nerve-wracking situations? Or are you the kind of person who immediately zeros in on the negatives?

Being an optimist and seeing the glass as half-full is not the same thing as wearing rose-colored lenses. This does not mean you disregard the stress in your life. Being an optimist simply means that you have taken the time to develop processes that allow you to cope with your emotions in a productive manner.

This way, you are less sad, depressed, or anxious, and you're often able to develop stronger relationships with other people.

On the other hand, being a pessimist does not mean that you are a realist. It simply means that you have not developed the mechanism needed to deal with emotions productively, and the ability to find the good in every bad.

Our Perception Determines
Our Experience

Once I attended a conference in Chicago. I was so amazed that the people I met there seemed to have completely different observations of the state in which they lived.

For example, when I asked what the winters were like in their town, I got very different answers from people depending on where they originally lived. When I asked the question of a former Californian, she talked as if she'd landed in Siberia, complaining about the snowfall and treacherous conditions meant for only the wildest of beasts. When I asked the same question of a native resident, he painted a beautiful picture of the changing seasons, each more spectacular than the last.

What's the difference here? Their perception dictated their experience.

This can be as simple as us perceiving a statement in a different way than it was intended.

I've experienced this in my relationships time and time again. My husband will say something to me like, "Would you mind putting your dirty plate in the dishwasher instead of leaving it in the sink?" But I hear, *You disgust me and can never do anything right. Are you stupid? Don't you know how to clean up after yourself?*

My husband was simply letting me know the dishwasher was dirty, and asking if I could put my dishes in there. That way, the sink wouldn't fill up with dirty dishes, creating a mess. No judgment, just a request. But my perception of the situation changed the way I experienced the encounter. Before I worked on the way I view my perceptions, I would always think the worst. *People don't like me. I suck.*

Why does this happen? Once again, our perception determines our experience.

It works like this: I bet at one time or another, we've all gone into a grocery store and noticed that everyone seemed happy, helpful, and cheery that day. Even the people in the checkout line were full of good spirits. Yet, when we've gone another day, we've had a completely different experience. We found people to be grumpy and in a bad mood—every one of them. It's possible that your experience was tainted by your state of mind. The first visit to the grocery store, you were happy and relaxed and not stressed. The second time, you may have had a fight with your spouse and were on edge. Things in your life were going badly so when you visited the store, every little thing was irritating. Your perception or tolerance of people in the store changed based on your feelings and how you view things.

I believe we view the outside world the same way we see ourselves. That's why many people continually attract drama into their lives while others do not, or why some people get into fights all the time while others refuse to let the same situation get the best of them.

If this is true, it explains a lot. It could be why, when we feel out of place and chaotic on the inside, we tend to attract more chaos and drama on the outside.

With that said, let me ask you the following questions:

What does your outside world look like right now? Are the people around you happy and productive? Are they full of life and passion, or do you find yourself in your own little tornado that seems to constantly bring nothing but negative energy your way? In other words, does it seem like everyone around you has problems and can never catch a so-called break?

Remember, you have the choice to work on your inner self to create a brighter outer self. Have you ever seen someone who has lost weight and noticed that they seem to have a new glow, or looked into someone's eyes just after their first child was born? There's a spark there, right?

Well, here's the good news. You have the ability to re-spark yourself.

Challenge: Take notice. That's it. I'm not asking you to do anything except become aware of how you're viewing things around you. By doing so, you'll find that when you're at your happiest, everyone else around you will be as well. On the flip side, if you want to know why the world seems to be crashing in on you, look inside, see what's out of place, and take the necessary action to repair it.

It's that simple. Because when it's all said and done, our perception determines our experience.

Playing to Win—Rethinking Our Perception of Success and Failure

Most people go through life playing *not to lose* rather than playing to win. The successful people in life are always playing to win. This is a choice, a mind-set. How do we get the mind-set of playing to win? We often have to let go of past conditioning. Most of us, from our earliest childhood days, were taught that failing is a bad thing. Playing not to lose is about playing it safe.

It is defense rather than offense. Playing not to lose is being afraid to fail.

Our society is so conditioned to see failure as a detrimental thing. You didn't get the job; you're a failure. You didn't win the game; you're a failure. You went out of business; you're a failure. If you look at people who have achieved extreme greatness, almost all of them had some major failings in their lives. If you ask them where they experienced the most growth, they will always say it was from their failures. I know this to be very true for me.

The failures I've personally experienced have added so much richness to my life. It took me three different attempts to finally succeed in business, for instance. All my previous failures taught me some valuable lessons about how to succeed, and they made the wins that much sweeter. For me, failure is taking a step backward in order to have the momentum to make that giant leap forward.

Whatever you are trying to achieve in life, it is worth doing a self-assessment to see if you are playing to win or playing *not to lose*. Is there anything holding you back from achieving your big dream? What beliefs do you hold about winning and losing that might be preventing you from taking that big step forward?

When you play to win, life becomes exhilarating! You feel better and become proud of yourself for all of your successes and achievements. You grow and are able to enjoy all the experiences you've been secretly desiring. Life becomes fun. You're no longer the one who sits on the sidelines. You are the powerful developer of your life.

Fun fact: There is magic in our perceptions. According to the way we perceive reality, our perceptions are constantly producing good and bad biochemical substances in our brain. Unless you clear up your negative or incorrect perceptions, you will create a tremendous amount of confusion for yourself. If you look at a problem in the right way, it's just a challenge. But if you look at a problem in the wrong way, *everything* becomes a problem.

Our perceptions can make us happy or sad. When we're happy, we produce all the good chemicals in our system. When we're miserable, we produce bad chemicals. All these substances affect our immune system, which is under the influence of our subconscious mind. Positive perceptions boost our immune system, and negative perceptions undermine and lower our immune system.

Since mental and physical health are so important to all of us for enjoyment of life, we should be looking at our perceptions and how we can change them to improve our health.

The moment we are born, our perceptions are conditioned by our external environment. As we grow up and gather different experiences, we are forced to change our perceptions. When young, we are naive and do a lot of dumb things under the influence of surging hormones; this is all part of learning. We think we're going to live forever and, therefore, life becomes one long adventure.

However, after a few knocks and bumps on the highway of life, reality sets in, and we realize that we are mortal after all. This forces our perceptions to change again. We look back and also philosophize about our future.

Learn from Your Bad Experiences
and Move Forward

Our lives are a constant series of experiences, both good and bad. We go through it all—awesome and terrible. It's a part of living.

Unless you are blessed with incredibly good luck, you will face disappointment and losses. You will be confronted by loneliness. You will run into problems that will, at first glance, seem to be bigger than you. But guess what? You are not alone.

For some reason, negative experiences are the ones that leave the greatest mark on us. When everything is right with our world, we are barely aware of our own existence or mortality, but then we are shattered when things don't go the way we expect them to. While optimists have a more positive outlook, almost everyone remembers negative things more strongly and in greater detail than the good happenings. There are psychological as well as physiological reasons for this.

First, the brain handles negative and positive information in different hemispheres. Negative emotions usually get us thinking more, and we tend to process negative happenings much more thoroughly than we process positive ones. Thus, it is part of human nature to contemplate more about unpleasant circumstances than happy ones. In fact, we even use stronger words to describe unhappy events than happy ones.

In 2001, Roy F. Baumeister, Ellen Bratslavsky, Catrin Finkenauer, and Kathleen D. Vohs explained in their coauthored scientific paper, *Bad Is Stronger than Good,* that we are impacted more by bad feedback, bad parents, and bad emotions than we are by good feedback, good parents, and good emotions. The authors also explained that it is easier to form bad impressions than it is to form good ones, and it is harder to disconfirm these bad impressions once they are formed.

This is why receiving criticism, being abandoned by friends, or losing money will have a greater impact than being praised, making new friends, or winning money.

Bad events also tend to wear off slower in our memories than the good ones. This is perhaps the reason why people remember unpleasant childhood memories more clearly than they remember the pleasant ones.

Fortunately, we have many more pleasant experiences than unhappy ones. That is a reality of life. Everything we experience, whether negative or positive, has a lesson somewhere inside of it if we look close enough. Some things about it worked and some did not. Certain aspects were enjoyable, and others were painful.

The objective should always be to learn from what happened. The more you take away from your experiences, the more you grow and the better equipped you become to deal with other situations in your future.

A life lesson is an authoritative piece of insight, knowledge, wisdom, or self-awareness that you implement to improve yourself, how you relate with people, and your life in general. The more life you experience, whether good or bad, the more lessons you accumulate.

What a beautiful gift life's lessons are! Unfortunately, they will not always arrive at our doorsteps with a Christmas bow. Sometimes, wisdom is found in the midst of tragedy, and we often discover life-changing lessons when we do not expect them. It is important to realize that they are priceless and worth treasuring at any time. The key is to use them as a guide to live life fully.

It's a hard pill to swallow, but try to remember that negative experiences are necessary experiences. They help us get our lives on track, learn to make better choices, and teach how to tell the difference between what we love and what we don't. All experiences, especially negative ones, make us better people. Ironic, I know.

You might not be able to control life experiences, but you have the power to control your reaction to such experiences. So, how do you benefit from negative experiences? Simple. Ask yourself, "What lesson did I learn?" Use that lesson to avoid bigger mistakes in your future.

When you view every experience as a life lesson, good or bad, you're able to accept what life is teaching you and can move beyond the pain that you feel in that moment.

Years ago, I invited a friend to partner with me on a project for my business. This was a business I had spent years building, and I was extremely proud of and passionate about it. The friend took me up on my offer. Stupidly, I didn't put any of the terms of our verbal agreement into a contract. For a while, everything seemed to be well. Business was good, and life was great. Until it wasn't.

Eventually, this friend wanted a larger cut of my business, yet didn't want to contribute time or money to help it grow, and things became strained between us. When I refused to give him a greater portion of my business that had nothing to do with him or the work he did for me, greed took over and he sued me for half a million dollars.

I was devastated. I couldn't believe that I invited a friend into my business—which made him tons of money—and he turned around and sued me. Like many other people would, I fell into a deep depression and got stuck in the *why me* mentality for too long. I wondered why bad things happened more to good people than they did to bad people. I had just been trying to help this friend. How on earth could he do this?

I tried coming to terms with this situation and moving on. However, I wasn't able to focus on advancing my business because I was stuck in a depression that was like a black hole. One day during this difficult time, I came across this passage by American mythology professor and author Joseph Campbell in his book, *A Joseph Campbell Companion: Reflections on the Art of Living*, where he explains Nietzsche's concept "the love of your fate":

> At a certain moment in Nietzsche's life, the idea came to him of what he called "the love of your fate." Whatever your fate is, whatever the heck happens, you say, "This is what I need." It may look like a wreck, but go at it as though it were an opportunity, a challenge. If you bring love to that moment—not discouragement—you will find the strength is there. Any disaster that you can survive is an improvement in your character, your stature, and your life. What a privilege! This is when the spontaneity of your own nature will have a chance to flow. Then, when looking back at your life, you will see that the moments which seemed to be great failures followed by wreckage were the incidents that shaped the life you

have now. You'll see that this is really true. Nothing can happen to you that is not positive. Even though it looks and feels at the moment like a negative crisis, it is not.

This passage helped me a great deal during my lawsuit. I printed it and carried it with me. Whenever I started feeling down and defeated, I would read it. If we try to view bad experiences as simply experiences, then those bad experiences become much easier to deal with.

I tried to think of the lawsuit as a learning experience. These are the life lessons that I learned:

1. I hadn't signed a contract with my friend because he was my friend, and I had erroneously believed the power of friendship would be greater than the lure of financial gain. Going forward after that experience, I never did business with anyone, no matter how close we were, without a contract guiding us. This lesson has helped me hold on to valuable friendships and relationships that money could have soured. It has also ensured that I never get the short end of the stick when it comes to relationships and business partnerships. I am *always* legally protected.

2. I started this business and built it from the ground up myself. Yet I offered this friend a fifty-fifty cut of my business. After that experience, I learned never to make that mistake again. Not only do I have a contract in place for all of my business relationships, I also will never offer someone half of what I worked hard for again. If we are building the business from scratch together, this is not a problem. But otherwise, no sir.

I believe that I wouldn't have learned these hard lessons if things had not gone this way. Would I have consciously chosen for the lawsuit to happen so I could learn these things? Of course not. But once it came to pass and our friendship was forever ruined, I could either choose to be bitter and devastated or learn from my mistake.

I chose to learn. If I hadn't accepted the hard lessons, perhaps I would have given even more of my business away for free in the future, or lost it completely. Who knows? What I *do* know is that, instead of letting this experience destroy me, I used it as a learning tool. It wasn't a bad experience that was happening to me because of fate. It was happening because some greedy idiot chose to become greedier. It was simply an experience. A really great learning experience.

By simply changing my perception, I changed the outcome of the experience.

Changing Your Views to Change Your Life

If you change the way you think about bad experiences, you can turn them into another notch on the belt of lessons learned. I'm not saying bad things don't happen, but what if we tried to change the way we handle those bad things?

Cognitive behavioral therapy (CBT) teaches us how to change the way we think about experiences and events. We can actually train our brains to view bad experiences as simply experiences and learning opportunities.

This is not training yourself to discount the fact that bad things happen. This is changing the way we think about those bad things and the control we give them over our lives.

Training your brain to view negative experiences differently isn't easy. But, if you are willing to acknowledge your feelings surrounding a negative event and work to change the way you view that event, then you can make a positive impact on your life and mental well-being.

CBT plays a vital role in changing the way we view negative experiences by helping us understand that our perception shapes our experiences. I may have the same experience as you, but my perception of that experience could be completely different. Remember our scenario of the half-full, half-empty glass of water?

CBT teaches us how to change the way we presently think about things. While some forms of psychotherapy focus on looking into the past to gain an understanding of current feelings, CBT shines a beam on our thoughts and beliefs in the present in contrast. It underlines the need to identify, challenge, and adjust how we interpret and perceive a situation.

CBT suggests the way people think can be likened to wearing a pair of glasses that forces you to see the world in a very specific way. The therapy works by making us aware of how these thought patterns influence our behavior and, in turn, create our reality.

For instance, someone who suffers from depression has distorted perceptions and interpretations. Living life with a warped view makes a person more vulnerable to a negative mind-set. This person may jump to conclusions fairly often and have a habit of viewing all events as catastrophic.

The aim of CBT is to transform the negative way that we think and behave, focusing on challenging these automatic thoughts and comparing them with reality. If you can change

your way of thinking, anguish decreases and you're able to function in a more beneficial way to yourself and others.

For example, someone with an extreme fear of dentists
because of a bad dental experience as a child may very well
believe that they will die in a dentist's chair. This is an irrational
thought, and a CBT therapist can work with this person to get
to the root of this defective thinking. For someone who always
sees the worst in every situation and struggles to learn a lesson
from that experience, CBT works to change the way he or she
sees things.

If you suffer from negativity in a crippling way, I encourage
you to find a qualified CBT professional to work with. In the
absence of one, there are many self-help courses and books that
aid you in changing the way that you think about and process
the happenings in your life. This book is one of those resources.

Actionable Ways to Change the Way Experiences Affect You

Regardless of our experiences, the biggest problems that
confront most of us are anger or an overwhelming sense of
sadness. These emotions have a way of dampening all other
emotions and pushing any solutions out of sight.

When you're experiencing intense anger or sadness, stop
and acknowledge why you are feeling the way you are. It helps
to write it down. Often, we don't want to think about what is
upsetting, so we try to ignore it, but the feelings are still there.
They fester and get worse because you aren't taking the time
to think through them. You may assume that by not thinking

about the issue, the negative feelings will eventually go away. It's possible, but not likely.

By evaluating the root of the feeling, you can overcome it. Oftentimes, our feelings are disproportionate to the cause. Try to extinguish your anger or sadness with deep breathing, meditation, long walks, or physical exercise. Any activity that calms you down will help.

Something else we often do when faced with negative challenges is to look for someone to blame. This includes finding ways to blame yourself—how you might have done things differently or not taken the path that you took to lead you to the here and now. This rarely leads to a positive result.

Accept what has happened. There's no changing that fact. What matters now is finding a solution to whatever mess that situation may have caused. Say you lose your job. You could dwell on the fact that you are now jobless and miserable, or you could accept it, take note of why it happened, and move on to find a new job. You cannot fix the problem until you accept what has happened.

What actually happened and what you think happened is not always the same thing. When we are stressed, worried, tense, or fearful, these emotions have a physical effect on us and lead us to mistake thoughts for facts. Taking the time to think objectively will offer us a better perspective on what we are feeling.

Get a piece of paper and document the experience that's causing these emotions.

- What happened? I am not asking you to write down your *feelings* about what happened. I am only asking you to write as factually and devoid of emotion as possible about what happened. For example,

I might write down, *My friend was short with me when I saw her on the street.*

- Write down your thoughts around that experience. For example, *I think I must have done something wrong, and my friend is mad at me.*
- Write down how you are feeling about what happened. For example, *I feel like my friend hates me, and that makes me sad. I am now hyper anxious and feeling depressed.*
- Now, write down a list of possible reasons for this experience that have nothing to do with you. For example, *My friend was late for work and stressed about making a meeting on time.*
- If the above reason is the true reason, then how does that feel? If you don't know the reason something happens, then make a list of other possibilities and pick the one that makes you feel less bad.

Now, let's assume your feelings are correct regarding this situation and you know the reason that it happened. You can still use this exercise. I'm going to use the example of my friend suing me.

- Write down what happened.
- Write down your thoughts.
  Example: *I messed up, and now this mistake is going to cost me thousands of dollars. I'm a failure.*
- Write down how you're feeling.
  Example: *I feel dumb, sad, stupid, and depressed. I will never recover from this mistake.*
- Write down a list of possible reasons this experience happened.
  Example: *This happened so I don't make a more catastrophic mistake in the future. This may have cost me thousands of dollars now, but I've learned a very valuable lesson. I will never make this*

mistake again, which may have saved me from losing my whole business and everything I own in the future.

- When you put this on paper, you are better able to see what you did wrong and how you can improve in the future. You can also see the things that were beyond your control and why you shouldn't blame yourself.

Contemplate what lessons this experience taught you and try to see it as an invaluable tool for the future. Any failure gives you a chance to correct things and grow as a person.

Once you have reminded yourself of the facts of the experience, take the time to write out the lessons you can learn from it. Commit to incorporating these lessons into your everyday life.

Studies show that putting down all of our negative thoughts on paper and destroying it afterward can drastically reduce the level of tension and stress that we feel as a result of such thoughts. You will find things become clearer when you write them down, and your feelings will not be as overwhelming.

Distract yourself by switching your brain over to study something different. This could involve developing a skill or playing a sport. New activity will gradually filter out the volume of unwelcome thoughts in your head. The same is true of physical exertion. As you distract yourself from the negative experience that has already taken place, you are empowered to move forward.

Constantly reliving the past means thinking about what could have been done or said differently until you feel like you're going crazy. Understand that doing this is no different than trying to go back a century to alter history.

If you have a superpower that allows you to travel back in time to change things, by all means set out on the journey and make things right. Odds are that you don't, so let it go. There is nothing you can do about it. Instead, examine yourself.

We often regret thinking about who we were before a bad experience soured us. However, you will give yourself the chance to become that person again when you allow yourself to remember who you used to be. Were you a loving person who saw the best in everyone? Even though someone has broken your trust, imagine yourself to still be that loving person who sees the best in everyone but perhaps scrutinizes people a little bit more.

Before my lawsuit, I was a giver. I willingly and happily gave my time, energy, and experiences to people. I wanted to share my successes with my friends so they could also succeed. After the lawsuit, I wanted to close my business and not open myself up to anyone, ever. I was miserable. I realized that I couldn't change what happened, I could only learn from it and move on. I was allowing the experience to affect my present-day happiness and mind-set, which ultimately would affect my future. I decided not to let that negative experience change who I am at the core. I continue to be a giver but am more cautious because of the lesson I learned. I let go of the bad and chose to learn, move on, and become a better person because of it.

The Ball Is in Your Court— What Will You Do with Your Experiences?

I have spent this chapter explaining how we can learn from our experiences, good or bad, and move on with life and the lessons learned. All this will mean absolutely nothing if you decide that your bad experiences are too overwhelming, too disastrous, or too exhausting for you to revisit.

The ball is fully in your court. There is nothing that I or a therapist can do for you if you are not willing to make the effort and do the work to change your thoughts and perceptions.

So, what will you do with that bad experience? Continue to label it as a bad experience and consume yourself with it? Or, simply see it as an experience full of lessons and do your best to learn from it?

Will you take it as an experience that is helping you to build your character? Or, will you fall under its weight?

It's your choice.

If you choose to learn the lessons from your experience and become a better version of yourself, I have a few tips for you:

1. Put on a positive lens and do all that you can mentally to change the way that you think about things. Challenge yourself to reframe circumstances in a more positive light than you used to.

2. Start a gratitude journal. I find this to be an excellent way of seeing the good in every aspect of life. Just before you go to bed every night, write down something positive that happened to you that day for which you are genuinely grateful. It doesn't have to be something earth-shattering. As you get into the habit of doing this, it can become hard to find new things to write. But, how about that great cup of coffee you started your day with? Or what about being able to pay some of your bills?

3. Be aware of the people you spend your time with. Hanging out with negative people will turn you into one. Conversely, spending your time with positive people will allow their positivity to rub off on you.

4. Turn off the news every once in a while. If you're in the habit
    of beginning your day with the morning news, which is almost
    always full of all the bad things that happened in the world the
    day before, you've already started with negativity. It's hard to
    stay positive when you are bombarded with discouraging news.
    Instead, consider doing some things that will have a positive effect
    on your mental health such as exercising, practicing mindfulness,
    or doing yoga. You can always catch up on the news later in the
    day once you've had a good start.

5. Learn to differentiate between the things you can control and the
    things you cannot. One of the great ways to eliminate or at least
    reduce stress is to acknowledge that there will be things that you
    can't control. For example, you cannot control what other people
    think of you or how they treat you. You can, however, control what
    treatment you will accept from people. And, decide not to worry
    about what others think.

Don't try to sweep the negatives under the rug. Experiences
happen that feel bad, but it makes no sense to ignore the real
world around you. The purpose of this book is to encourage
you to navigate life with a combination of realistic thinking and
optimism. Acknowledge the terrible experiences you've had,
glean the lessons they teach, and face the future armed with
those lessons.

CHAPTER TEN

Overcoming Rejection

We may encounter many defeats
but we must not be defeated.

—Maya Angelou

Have you ever thought to yourself, *I wish I didn't feel this way,* or *I wish I were less sensitive,* or *I wish I didn't take things so personally*? Odds are you have. Experiencing rejection leaves you full of insecurity and self-doubt, but it doesn't have to be this way. Now is the time to make a conscious change to help yourself feel more secure and take back your confidence, but how do you start?

To live a full and happy life, we must go after the things that matter to us: relationships, career, friendships, and so on. However, when reaching for the things that we want, we need to accept that there is always the possibility of rejection.

The reality is that rejection affects us all. In fact, for most people, rejection and the fear of rejection are perhaps the most distressing and impactful of life's experiences. We typically feel rejection during the hardest in emotional relationships, such as in friendships, families, romantic couples, and the professional sphere (especially in terms of career advancement).

Because of the negative feelings that accompany rejection, humans are naturally wired to avoid it. The opposite of rejection, the desire for acceptance, is a driving force that keeps many of us from being our most authentic selves. At times we are so driven by the need for acceptance that we, in the process, lose our personal and unique identities.

While rejection hurts, it is nearly impossible to avoid altogether and you shouldn't want to. Being irrationally afraid of rejection will hold you back from going after what you really want in life. The bid to avoid rejection at all costs will cause you to miss out on a lot of things because you are too afraid to try.

This is why, the better we get at handling rejection, the less it affects us. Rejection might be a harsh reality check, but if approached properly, it can be a tool to help nudge you in a direction that is better for you, your personality, your talents, and all the fantastic things that make you *you*.

Facing Rejection

There is a group of sales professionals who have learned how to handle rejection with ease. Notice that I did not say *ignore* rejection or *avoid* rejection, I said *handle* rejection. That means they are still experiencing it, but they have made rejection useful and put it in its rightful place.

T. Harv Eker, author of *Secrets of the Millionaire Mind*, knew that he would face enormous rejection in his climb up the wealth ladder. He decided to meet it head-on and took a job for two months as a telephone solicitor. He believed he would become numb to rejection, and he was correct. People hung up on him, swore at him, called him names, blew loud whistles into the phone, and tore him and his offer to shreds. He never felt so despised.

And he was thrilled because of it.

He knew that he could never handle rejection without actually experiencing it. A *lot* of it. Like any skill, it takes practice and you can only get better with lots and lots of it.

The only way to get used to something is to actually experience it and move through it until it doesn't affect you anymore. Those sales professionals and people who overcome rejection understand that working through it is what gives them self-confidence. They don't fear it. They embrace it.

If you avoid rejection, you'll stay neat and clean and won't muss yourself, much like a china doll that sits quietly on the shelf. Or, you can be a Raggedy Ann. They get messy and stepped on and thrown around the room, but they're also the ones having all the fun.

Rejection Comes in Many Forms

We may experience rejection in any of these ways:

Family rejection. Rejection from your family, whether from a parent, sibling, grandparent, child, or any other relative, can be devastating. It manifests itself as withholding affection and love, neglect, abuse, or outright abandonment. Because family is supposed to be forever, and these are the people who should have your back no matter what, this form of rejection is likely to haunt the person throughout life if not properly confronted.

Rejection from a friend. Friendships are often powerful relationships, but the reality is that people's opinions about each other sometimes change. Whether due to the passage of time, new life experiences, or other reasons, there will be times in your life that someone just won't want to be your friend anymore, and this can be painful.

Romantic rejection. When we speak about rejection, this is the form that many people immediately call to mind because it is often the most shattering of all rejection. When we are in love with someone, or believe that we are, rejection by that person can make us feel like there is nothing worth living for anymore.

Almost all of us will experience romantic rejection at least once, unless you are a very lucky person. We may love someone who doesn't love us in quite the same way. We may end up with a partner who withholds intimacy or affection or someone might break up with us, leaving us alone and devastated. We may ask a crush to go on a date and be snubbed, or the one we thought we'd spend forever with suddenly tells us that he or she wants a divorce.

Work-related rejection. This may happen at a job that you already work at and entail team leaders or seniors choosing someone else over you, not getting the promotion you deserve, losing out to a competitor on sales, not getting that sought-after assignment, or being denied a salary raise. Work-related rejection can also happen at the point of searching and being passed over for a new job.

Each form of rejection affects us in different ways, and therefore we must treat each of them differently. The following sections will discuss different forms of rejection and what we can do to overcome them.

Family Rejection

On the pain scale of life, many could argue that death is the number one cause of anguish. I would argue that rejection by those who are supposed to love you is at the top of life's pain scale. Death hurts your heart. Rejection damages your soul.

As sad and painful as it is to experience the death of a loved one, their death can never be misconstrued as a personal attack. The person who died did not do so to spite you, and even in the throes of grief, you know this. With time, the hurt you feel eases.

When you face rejection from a loved one, it can hardly be taken as anything other than a personal attack. Repeated rejection changes the ways you view yourself and perceive how others view you. It can negatively affect the choices and decisions you make throughout your life.

I've experienced painful loss. My mother was my best friend, and her death was sudden and unexpected. When she died, a piece of my heart went with her. Grief ravaged me for a long time, but as the years passed, the loss became less painful. I still miss her terribly, and my heart will always hurt for that loss, but I live my life with the happy memories my mom brought to it.

I have also faced rejection—terrible rejection from people I grew up with thinking they loved me. *That* rejection haunts me daily. It affects the ways I view myself and interact with other people. I will share my story of rejection with you, along with my strategies for accepting rejection for what it truly is and not allowing it to control my life.

Growing up adopted, I always felt "giveaway-able," like I had been rejected by my birth parents. Even though I know it must have been a difficult decision to give me up for adoption, I still grew up feeling that rejection. I was always curious about who they were and if they had other children they decided to keep. When I turned twenty-two, I searched for them. With the help of city hall records, I found a couple who I was convinced were my birth grandparents. I wrote them a letter explaining who I was and that I thought I might be their birth granddaughter. If this was true, I asked them to please give the letter to my birth mother. I thanked her for having the strength to give me up and let her know that I was doing okay in life—I was successful and educated, and I didn't want anything from her. I just wanted the chance to let her know I was okay and to get some answers about my genetic background. In my letter to my birth grandparents, I sent a self-addressed stamped envelope and asked if they would please put my envelope back in the mail to me if I'd contacted the wrong people so I'd know that my letter simply didn't get lost.

About two weeks after I sent my letter, I received a letter back from my birth grandparents. The first line said, "Yes, you've found the right people, and we've been waiting for your letter for four years." I was overjoyed and began sobbing. It was like my muscles had been tense for twenty-two years, and they just decided to relax at that moment. They told me my birth parents broke up shortly after having me, but then years later, they got back together and married. This could not have worked out any better. I didn't have to worry about a spouse that didn't want her to have contact with me, or worse, that didn't know about me. I knew for sure that they'd want to meet me!

Two days later, I received a letter from my birth brother. He had been snooping in their room for money and came across my letter. Everything I had described sounded true to him, and he believed that I was his sister. He sent me pictures and told me he had a younger brother and that he was so excited to have a sister. Life, at that moment, was amazing. My birth parents married each other, my grandparents had been waiting for me to contact them, and my birth brother was super excited to have a sister … *and* I had pictures! I could finally see what my birth parents looked like. It was so strange and cool how much I looked like my birth brothers.

Two days after receiving my birth brother's letter, the self-addressed stamped envelope I had sent in my original letter to my birth grandparents came back empty! I was devastated and confused. I called my grandparents and told them, and they said my birth parents were very angry. They never thought I'd contact them, and they didn't want anything to do with me. They told my grandparents not to have contact with me either.

My birth parents didn't know my grandparents and brother wrote to me. So, instead of sending me a kind letter saying I found the right people yet they couldn't deal with being in touch with me, they just mailed my envelope back empty. This would have made me think I didn't find them, and I would have spent the rest of my life searching and always coming up empty.

As if things couldn't get any worse, I received an actual letter from my birth parents days later. They had discovered that my birth brother wrote to me and were furious. The letter said to leave them and their family alone and not to contact them again. They couldn't deal with seeing me and may never be able to deal with it.

To be rejected in that way was beyond devastating. If people who got pregnant as teenagers out of love and later married one another didn't want to see me, then they really had discarded me. I was not worth keeping. I was not worth knowing. I felt worthless and let this destructive rejection rule my life.

Growing up as an adopted child, there were people in my life who didn't accept me as their *true* family. For example, at Christmas, my father's parents would give all the grandkids twenty dollars but would only give five dollars each to me and my brother. In their eyes, we weren't blood-related and, therefore, not really family. They treated us like neighbor kids.

Even family members who treated us better still made us feel like we weren't *true* family members. I had a cousin say to me one time that he loved me "like family." Like family! What? *I am family*. He should have just said, "I love you." It was these little rejections that tore me down.

Being rejected by your adopted family and again by your birth family is devastating. I had to find ways to get over the feelings I was having and how I viewed and treated myself as a result of those rejections.

There is no way around it, rejection sucks. And, unfortunately, there is no way to avoid being rejected in life. What you can do is find ways to live with it without allowing it to negatively affect other areas of your life.

Looking back at my life, I can now recognize how

experiencing those rejections affected my interpretations and reactions toward other people. I never felt good enough. I went into every relationship, even with employers and colleagues, having the idea that they would not like me. I saw this as a way to protect myself. *I know they won't like me, so I won't be upset when I find out they don't like me.* And when they did show me acceptance, I never truly believed it. I always felt that they would wake up one day and realize that I wasn't actually worthy of being liked, and they'd reject me.

Over the years, I created negativity in my life because I was always anticipating rejection. I often wonder how life would have been different for me if I had viewed some relationships without my rejection goggles on, if I didn't always have a wall up.

How to Deal with Family Rejection

Talk it out. If possible, have a sit down with the family member who has been rejecting you and have a discussion about the root of the problem. Talk about how you feel hurt and rejected. Don't be accusatory. Simply state how his or her actions make you *feel*. Sometimes family members don't even know they are treating you in a way that you perceive to be hurtful. With my family member that said, "I love you *like* family," I should have told him that it hurts when he says, *like* family. He should love me because I am family. I'm sure he didn't even realize his word choice made me feel rejected.

Don't assume people can read your mind. You have to communicate. Sometimes writing a letter or email is better than sitting down and having a face-to-face conversation. It can be a difficult topic to broach, and the person you are talking to may feel attacked and defensive. If you take the time to explain it in writing, then you are able to formulate your thoughts well and give them time to digest what you are trying to communicate. Talking to the family member may work and it may not, but it's a good place to start.

Give it time. Speaking to this person may not make things better overnight. This is because emotions such as resentment, frustration, and anger are sometimes so high that civil discussions will not work. If this is the case, you might want to wait until things have settled down a bit.

People don't always take it well when their hurtful actions are pointed out to them. It can be hard to swallow being told you are doing something that is causing someone pain. Give the person space to absorb what you have told him or her.

Don't expect change overnight. If they do something that bothers you, point it out in the moment in a nonconfrontational way. Not everything has to be an argument. If they do something, simply say, "I hope you don't mind me pointing this out, but when you do this or say that, it makes me feel…" Hopefully, the person will be open to learning and changing behaviors. If they have been treating you this way for a long time, it may be difficult. Give it time, but set an end date where you will no longer allow yourself to be treated in a way that makes you feel rejected. If they keep it up, it's okay to leave.

Visit a family counselor. If both of you are willing to work on your relationship but don't know how, it makes sense to involve a third party. A family counselor can objectively examine both points of view and present possible resolutions. If you cannot afford it or are not too comfortable with a family counselor, enlist a trustworthy relative or close family friend who can bring objectivity to the table.

Set boundaries and protect them fiercely. At the end of the day, it is your job to teach your family how to treat you. Just like you would do when dealing with a toxic family member, you need to protect your own mental well-being when you feel rejected. Instead of taking your family member's rejection personally and dwelling on their treatment of you, set a boundary that you expect respect and acceptance. By setting boundaries, you control the narrative surrounding the perceived rejection. They aren't rejecting you; you are rejecting their treatment of you. Let your family member know what you will and won't take from them as well as what will happen if your boundaries aren't respected.

Leave, but leave with love. Letting go of a relationship that has rejected you shows great self-esteem and self-love. However, I want to encourage you to try your best to never let your final words be angry ones. Don't slam the door in finality and nail it shut with angry words because we never can tell what the future holds. There are many people on their deathbeds who wish they hadn't severed a family relationship so completely. Don't leave room for this kind of regret. Express yourself and leave nothing unsaid, but don't be so mean that there is no hope for the future. People change, and this family member might change too.

Take care of yourself. In the aftermath of severing a family relationship, you will feel emotional pain even if you were the one who chose to walk away. It is important to take care of yourself during this time. Don't neglect to eat healthy and exercise.

Engage in calming activities that keep you grounded and less anxious.

Understand that healing might take a while. Even though it sounds cliché, time does help. You will not be able to predict or rush the healing. You might feel good about yourself and your decisions for a little while. Then you might feel down for a little bit after that. It is okay. Healing from rejection is often not a straight road but rather a curved road with several twists and turns. Embrace it all with the full understanding that healing will eventually come.

Romantic Rejection

If you have never been dumped before, you're lucky. It sucks. There is no way to sugarcoat the feelings you have when someone you love doesn't love you back. When the person doesn't want to be with you, you begin to wonder what's wrong with you. Was it something you did or said? Was it something you didn't do or say? You may feel unlovable and begin to question if you'll ever find *the one*.

The reality is if the person doesn't want to be with you, then you don't have to change who you are to make them want to be with you. Spend time and energy on finding someone who will love you for you. It may hurt being rejected, but it will pass if you choose to open yourself up to other opportunities.

In chapter five, I discussed ending toxic relationships. Even though I'm the one who ultimately left my ex-husband, there was a level of rejection I faced with him. He rejected the idea of moving to another place with me so he wouldn't have access to gambling machines. I had to deal with him choosing to continue his lifestyle without making any sacrifices to be with me. The feeling of rejection in that relationship was strong, and it made me insecure moving forward.

Even though I felt devastated at the time, it was a huge blessing in disguise. After I recovered from the loss, I opened myself up to love again and met my amazing husband.

How to Deal with Romantic Rejection

While romantic rejection is not the easiest thing in life to deal with, we need to understand that romantic rejection is part and parcel of dating. We won't always be able to avoid rejection, but we can use those rejections to build ourselves into the person we want to be.

Here are methods you can use to get over romantic rejection:

Be graceful. Yes, it may feel like you are about to die or want to explode with hate all over the person rejecting you. However, it is better that you act with dignity and not lash out, no matter how distraught you may feel inside. Be graceful and courteous, and leave on a civil note. Taking the high road isn't always easy, but you'll thank yourself when you can look back on the breakup and be proud of how you handled it.

Don't take it too personally. It is pretty hard not to take a romantic rejection personally, but the key is not to take it *too* personally. You have to force yourself to remember, even when it is hard, that the rejection is not a commentary on you as a person. Perhaps they are looking for something else in a partner or are just not ready for the complications of a romantic relationship at this point in their lives. And, you must remember that romantic relationships *are* complicated. Whatever their reason for the rejection, try to understand that most of them will be entirely outside your control.

Don't apportion blame. Don't blame the other person for the rejection. Yes, you'll feel pain and grieve. Try to remember that, while they might have hurt you, they most likely weren't trying to do so intentionally. It is natural to feel attacked when we are hurt, and it is also important to understand that romantic rejections aren't always about wrongdoing or an attack.

Allow yourself to grieve. Losing a relationship can feel a little like death. This is the death of the dreams of the future you pictured with this other person. You will feel sad, and you must permit yourself to grieve what you have lost. Following the rejection, you will have good days, and you will have bad days. Feel your feelings because they are yours to feel.

Stay away. This is most crucial if you had a solid relationship with this person before now. Giving yourself the freedom to grieve entails cutting off any contact with this person, at least for a while. Constantly being near the person will not allow you to properly deal with what you are feeling.

Don't get in touch. Even when you are trying to stay away, you will sometimes be tempted to call the person. If you believe there is no hope of any friendship with this person in the future, delete their number. If you must relate with the person in the future—perhaps, you share custody of a child—you might want to hide their number for a while so as not to fall prey to the temptation to text or call them when you are particularly down.

Try something new. If your daily routine reminds you about this person, disrupt your pattern and try something new. This could be going to different restaurants than the one you two used to go together. Try out a new hobby. If you shared friends, you might want to seek out friends who don't know the two of you as a couple.

Make time for other relationships that you have. Remember that your life is not circumscribed to your romantic relationship only. This is the time to strengthen other relationships with your family and friends. Be social and invest in other people. It is, however, vital that you take the time to invest in your relationships whether you are in a romantic one or not, and whether you are going through a romantic break up or not. It is the friends that you took time to make and remain friends with who may very well be your salvation when you experience a breakup.

Get out there again. Let me assure you, the grieving will eventually subside, and once you have taken the time to build yourself up, *please* get back out there. Romantic relationships are complicated, but they also make life more fulfilling. I am not asking you to fall in love with the next prospect. At least go out to lunch with someone new. One rejection isn't, and shouldn't, be taken as a life sentence.

Friendship Rejection

Rejection from a friend can hurt almost as bad as rejection from a romantic partner or as much as rejection from a family member. I had a teaching partner who became my best friend. We did everything together, and I loved her like family.

Then one day, she got a new boyfriend and, almost overnight, she dumped me. I was happy for her that she was finally in a loving relationship because she deserved that. I gave her space to be with him. When relationships are new, your blinders go up on everything else. You just want to spend all your time getting to know this new and exciting person in your life.

If your friend ditches you for a guy, give her space at first. Don't take it personally. She isn't ditching you; she's choosing to spend her free time getting to know this new person. However, when months go by and things don't change, that's when you may start feeling rejected.

My old teaching partner became friends with her boyfriend's friends, and began to spend all of her time with them. She allowed her old friends to be pushed aside. It hurt. When I started dating my husband, we always included her in any activities we were doing. We spent New Year's Eve together, went camping together, she joined us at concerts and parties, and so on. She was part of our lives.

When she started dating her boyfriend, we no longer mattered to her. There was no talk of ending the friendship; she just fazed me out. This form of rejection can be damaging because you can't necessarily mourn the moment of rejection. It happens slowly and painfully over a period of time. It's like pulling off a Band-Aid so slowly that it pulls each and every single hair out one by one.

How to Deal with Rejection from a Friend

If it does happen to you, here are a few ways to deal with rejection from a friend:

Take the time to cool off. While your instincts may tell you otherwise, please know that it is a good idea not to try and force it with a friend who has rejected you. You always want to be the bigger person, and odds are that you will not be this person if you reach out to them in your anger or sadness. As much as you can, do not try to hurt them back, no matter how satisfying you might imagine that would feel.

Own and feel your emotions. There is no right or wrong way to feel when suffering from rejection from a friend. You may be angry, or you may be sad. Both of these emotions are valid. Allow yourself to feel whatever it is you are feeling.

Don't badmouth that friend to others. If you have mutual friends, don't speak ill of the person who rejected you. It will make those friends uncomfortable, and you will come across as petty. It may push them away in the process. You don't want to create more rejection in your life. As I mentioned earlier, taking the high road is harder, but it's the road that will take you further in life. Be the better person.

Surround yourself with positive people. As much as you can, surround yourself with people who are helpful, positive, and make you feel good about yourself. Just because one friend stopped being friends with you doesn't mean that others won't enjoy your company. If you'd like to take the time to be alone, by all means, do so. Enjoy your own company if that's what you'd rather do, but don't alienate yourself from others and invite more rejection into your life.

Work on your self-esteem. The loss of a friendship can do a number on your self-esteem if you are not careful. You wonder what it is about you that made this friend stop liking you. This is the time to remind yourself of just how great a person you are. Make a list of your accomplishments if you feel that will help. Remind yourself of the good things you have going for you. Reassure yourself that the loss of this friendship does not mean the loss of you.

Don't take it personally. Here we go again. More often than not, rejection feels very personal. But, it is not always so. Interests change, and so do goals and values. Have you considered the fact that your friend no longer shares your common interests or doesn't have the same values as you?

Even if the rejection was personal, so what? Just because this person doesn't appreciate or like certain things about you doesn't mean that other people will feel the same way. The friend speaks only for his- or herself.

Get reflective. Whether positive or negative, all experiences have a lesson to teach us. Rejection has its own peculiar lessons, too, and you will do yourself a world of good to reflect on your experience so that you can grow as an individual.

Don't let this stop you from making new friends. No one ever said that you can't or won't have more than one meaningful friendship in your life, so go ahead and cultivate more friendships. Explore activities that you enjoy, and you'll be sure to make new friends there. Remember, one rejection is not the end of the world.

Job Rejection

In our society, this type of rejection can often feel as damaging as a personal rejection. Although you have a superb résumé and the interview seemed perfect, you may not get the job. You will face rejection as part of the job search, and there are two things to keep in mind when you're not offered the job.

First, there may be more candidates than jobs. More than

ever, the job search requires more from the applicants. Most likely, you will send out a higher number of résumés than ever before; you will have fewer interviews than ever before; and, you will face rejection more frequently. This frustrating situation can often be the result of a weak economy and a shattered job market.

It is also essential to remember that this type of rejection is not personal. You are riding the *rejection boat* in the company of many competent, experienced, and talented applicants.

So, when rejection comes, and it will, what should you do? Perform an attitude check and choose to handle this minor setback with a positive attitude. If you need an attitude adjustment, quickly work on it. Use this rejection as a learning tool. Honestly review your résumé or have a trusted associate critique it for you. It might need a few tweaks to just help it pop.

Review the interview process. Were you on time and prepared? Was your appearance appropriate for the job? Were there any "oh no" moments in your mind during or after the interview? Maybe you could have provided better responses or asked better questions. It is not the end of the world. Use this experience to make the next interview stronger. Do some additional research and rehearse for a more focused interview.

If you are rejected for a job:

Don't take it personally. You mustn't take a job rejection as a personal condemnation, with the full understanding that there is so much competition in the professional world and employers will make a decision based on who they believe is best suited for the role. So, don't think the HR person made a conscious vote *against* you. He or she simply made a conscious vote *for* someone else.

Get feedback that will help you in the future. While not all hiring managers will give you a clear idea of why you didn't get this job, some will. This is why it is important to ask for constructive feedback as to why you didn't get a job offer. There could very well be a good reason you were overlooked, such as gaps in your skill set. Being able to receive feedback about this may give you a huge leg up in your future applications.

Focus on your strengths. Yes, you have room for improvement. You must not forget, however, that you still bring your own unique selling points to the table. Remind yourself of your strengths, as focusing on these can imbue you with a renewed sense of energy and the momentum required to find the right job for you. Make a list of your contributions to previous employers as well as a list of your strengths. These lists will not only give you confidence but can also be handy for your next job interview.

Look for areas that need improvement. How do you present yourself to others, especially in formal situations? How professional are your résumé and cover letter? How do you answer key interview questions? How do you speak? Take a crucial look at all these and then work on the areas that need improvement.

Don't lose your momentum. While waiting to hear back about that dream job you interviewed for, it is important not to lose your momentum in your quest for employment even if you might not really feel like looking for other jobs. Maintain contact with your recruitment professionals, and don't forget to stay in touch with your network. This kind of preemptive approach helps to keep your self-esteem up. More importantly, it stops you from putting all your hopes on a job that might not pan out.

The question that haunts everyone after a rejection is, "But, why?" It is possible that another candidate had more education or experience and better qualifications than you. Or, maybe you were just spared a miserable work environment. We all want to believe that everyone likes us, but it is possible that there was a lack of chemistry during the interview. Would you really want to work for someone who had a negative attitude toward you?

Everyone would like the answer to "But, why?" Accept the fact that you will probably never know the reason for the rejection. View this as an opportunity to improve, grow, and learn. You are in control, and you have the option to stay positive. You can go forward stronger and better prepared. The perfect job is waiting for you and may be just an interview away!

How to Deal with Career Rejection

Career rejection can come in the form of being passed over for a promotion you feel you deserve, not getting the big account you know you're qualified to work on, or asking for a raise and being turned down. All of these situations can feel like a slap to the face. However, there are ways to handle career rejection and become a stronger person for it.

If you are rejected for a position in your workplace:

Manage your emotions. Facing rejection in the workplace may cause you to experience a shift in your personality and perspective, and it is important to watch that your emotions don't get in the way of professionalism. For example, while engaging someone in a heated argument might seem appealing at the moment when you are overlooked for a sought-after assignment, it is likely that it might cause your superiors to label you as unprofessional. You don't want to give the impression that you are unable to deal with competition, tough conversations, and high pressure, as this might affect your prospects, future growth, performance, and career opportunities within that company. Don't react impulsively. Calm yourself by taking a few deep breaths before considering the best course of action.

Sleep on it. If you would like to respond to the rejection, I recommend sleeping on it before approaching anyone at the company. You might want clarification as to why you didn't get the promotion. You might just want to say something on the topic. Whatever it may be, sleeping on it will help you come at the rejection from a fresher and calmer perspective.

There have been times in my life where I was upset with someone or something at work, and I penned a very angry email. I always waited until the next day to send it because I knew that with a fresh mind, I would approach the email differently. Sleeping on it will save you from acting impulsively and regretfully.

Assess the situation. I encourage you to take any workplace rejection as an opportunity to reassess your strengths and weaknesses. More often than not, workplace rejections are impartial and unintentional. Perhaps the other person had more experience or education, or they just had better human relation skills. Take a moment to reflect on whether your behavior or actions have led to the rejection in any way and learn the lessons that are presented to you from this rejection.

Ask for feedback. Once you have gotten your emotions

under control, the next best thing you can do is seek feedback and clarification as to why you didn't get the promotion, raise, or assignment. Don't weave stories in your head. Instead, discuss the issue with human resources, your boss, or the superior involved so that you can have a rounded view of what actually happened. You must be open to criticism and take it constructively. When you seek feedback in this way, do not argue, defend yourself, or blame others. This will defeat the whole purpose of you asking for clarification.

Loving Yourself When You Feel Rejected

When we feel the blow of major rejection—the betrayal of a close friend, a wound from a family member, the unfaithfulness of a mate—we may wonder if we'll ever get over the hurt. As we try to make sense of our pain, we can be tempted to respond to rejection in destructive ways.

Generally, what do you do when you feel rejected? If you're like most people, you either try to control the rejecter, or you take it out on yourself with various avoidant and controlling behaviors. It's important to understand how you react to rejection. This will help you begin to make positive changes that will allow you to still value yourself when you feel rejected. It helps to write down your answers to these questions to give you a better understanding of your actions and reactions.

When you try to control the other person, do you try to control by:

- Getting angry, defending, complaining, blaming?

- People-pleasing, complying, giving yourself up?
- Shutting down, withdrawing?
- Threatening violence or exposure?

When you take it out on yourself, do you try to control yourself and/or your feelings by:

- Harshly judging and criticizing yourself?
- Avoiding your feelings by ruminating, justifying, or turning to various addictions, such as food, alcohol, drugs, television, shopping?
- Seeing yourself as a victim and complaining to others?
- How do you feel when you exhibit any of these controlling behaviors toward the other person or yourself? Are you:
  > Anxious?
  > Depressed?
  > Angry?
  > Alone?
  > Empty?
  > Shamed?
  > Guilty?
  > Resentful?

When rejected, we often feel self-contempt, which means we take the full responsibility for the rejection. We wonder, *What is it about me that causes people to reject me? Is there something so repulsive that no one wants me?* This mentality is self-destructive and will hinder you from moving past the rejection. Recognize that most rejections are not personal. The first step to let go of self-contempt is to know your worth and love yourself.

Loving yourself should start long before someone rejects

you and begins with not rejecting yourself. If you are reject-ing yourself, you won't be able to love yourself when you feel rejected by another.

Loving yourself starts by defining your intrinsic worth. This means not defining your worth by your looks, your achieve-ments, or by how others feel about you, but seeing and valuing your beautiful self—your natural kindness, caring, compassion, creativity, and goodness as well as your gifts, talents, and unique intelligence.

When you value who you are within, then it's much easier not to take others' rejection personally. After my birth parents rejected me, I hated them, I hated myself, and I hated life. It took me a long time to figure out that their rejection of me had more to do with their feelings about themselves and less to do with how they felt about me. There are still times when I lapse back into those feelings of rejection, but I try to be mindful in those moments and work to not let my negative self-talk get me down.

Learn the Lessons of the Rejection, and Move On to Better Things

Though it might not seem like it, rejection should motivate you to do better. If you look at any rejection that you suffer as an opportunity to become a better version of yourself, it can actually be a plus rather than a negative.

If you feel like you're constantly being rejected, despite doing your best to correct your mistakes, it's time to seek some unbiased advice. The truth is we all have blind spots that require other people's outlook. If you have a trusted relative or friend, and you are willing to accept their criticism, ask for their opinion. If you have access to a professional who can help you work through your feelings of rejection, please do.

When you've heard the same information over and over again from different people, in different contexts, it is time to listen. Use this feedback to assess and evaluate yourself so that you can do better in the future. I have heard countless stories of people's lives, careers, and relationships taking the turn for the better only after rejection. Some people get to meet the love of their lives because they were rejected by someone they had a crush on. Others move on to the job of their dreams because a company turned them down and forced them to reevaluate what they really enjoy doing. Whatever the rejection is, let it drive you to make a change for the better.

Rejection can teach us patience and remind us of our humanness, though it hurts at the onset. Understand that you won't always get what you want right away, but that if you will be patient and put in the hard work, you'll eventually reach your goals.

We all get tunnel vision once in a while, and we spend the entirety of our days focusing on one dream, one person, or one job to the exclusion of all else. You can use rejection as a tool to look around with new eyes and consider how to view your goals and dreams. Let this rejection motivate you to explore different paths. There might be an alternative path you need to take that you would not have given a second glance in the past. Sometimes rejection is nature's way of nudging us on a different path.

Even though rejection can often feel like the end—the end of a relationship, the end of a career path, or the end of how we thought our lives would turn out—the truth is, rejection opens up the opportunity for something better to begin. We don't often grow when everything is working for us. Growth really only occurs when we are forced to cope with the undesirable or the unexpected, aka rejection.

Yes, rejection can be painful, but you have the choice of viewing it as a blessing in disguise. So, the question is this: Will you take this rejection as an opportunity to be better, or will you allow it to break you?

CHAPTER ELEVEN

It's Okay to Ask for Help

*Asking for help does not
mean that we are weak or incompetent.
It usually indicates an advanced level
of honesty and intelligence.*

—Anne Wilson Schaef

So many of us have a hard time asking for help for fear that we're going to seem weak or lose control. We may be embarrassed or ashamed of needing help and may not know what to ask for. Some people don't even realize they need help.

For those of us who had to be self-sufficient from an early age, with parents or guardians who were not available to help us through our dark times, physically and emotionally, asking for help might not feel natural. Why ask for help as adults when we have spent the entirety of our lives taking care of ourselves?

Fear is perhaps one of the most debilitating emotions a human can feel, and it is one of the reasons many of us choose to stay in a rut rather than ask for help. We feel like asking for help and being told no is a negation of ourselves, that our vulnerability will be equated with weakness, and that we will be exposed as frauds in the positions that we hold.

Holding on to these false beliefs can make it hard to reach out for help. Many individuals wrongly believe that asking others to listen or to help is nothing but a waste of those people's time.

Low self-esteem can also be an obstruction on the road to help. Someone with low self-esteem does not value his or her own needs and is more likely to put the needs of other people before their own. This kind of person is also often hard on him- or herself and will interpret asking for a helping hand as further validation of that weakness or inferiority.

Pride can also impede a person's ability to ask for help. Doing things by yourself is very satisfying, and it can become a habit, even when you are failing and clearly need assistance.

Finally, we do not like to ask for mental help because we instinctually avoid dredging up past traumas. Most of us have had at least one negative experience in the past that hurt us badly. We know asking for help will force us to confront that trauma, and we don't want to relive the pain all over again.

However, when we refuse to ask for help, we are stuck facing problems on our own and oftentimes almost collapsing under the weight of those problems.

Making the admission that you need therapy or help for your mental health can be hard because a lot of us equate our minds with who we are. The reasoning is that an unhealthy mind means that you are not as good as others, less than ideal, broken, and fundamentally weak. Even though things are better than they used to be, mental health issues are still hugely stigmatized.

Taking the Stigma out of Mental Health Issues

Sadly, many people who deal with mental health issues have been blamed for their problems. How many times have you been told to just breathe, that you can control this if only you tried harder, or that it is just a phase and that you will outgrow it?

Unfortunately, stigmatizing the need for mental health brings embarrassment where there should be none and causes people to bear shame for things they cannot control. People then avoid seeking the help they need.

Yes, the stigma has been reduced in recent years, but the pace of progress has not been quick enough to help everyone.

How can you personally take the stigma out of mental health issues?

Don't self-isolate. It is natural to want to hide a mental issue from people and to isolate yourself simply because you feel that no one will understand. Don't. Talk to your family, friends, your doctor, or anyone else that you can trust for compassion and support.

Understand that you are not weak. Sometimes, the stigma is not just from external sources. Too often, we make the error of believing that what we are feeling makes us weak, that we should be able to control ourselves. This is not the case. You aren't weak because you admit to the fact that you are struggling emotionally. It takes great strength to be self-aware and courageous enough to seek the help you need.

Get treatment. Don't be reluctant to admit that you need treatment. Put on your armor of courage and step out. Do not allow small-minded people's incorrect opinions to stop you from getting relief from the problems interfering with your life.

You are not your illness. Never ever think you are nothing more than your illness. You are not an illness, and your vocabulary should show this. You are not depression. You struggle with depression, but you can beat it. It isn't who you are. These are two very distinct statements that make a difference in your thought process.

Join a support group. There are various local and national support groups that offer resources for people dealing with mental issues. Ask your doctor or therapist for a good group recommendation that they think would be beneficial to you and attend at least one meeting to see if it helps. You would not believe how cathartic it can be hearing from others who are experiencing the same thing you are. Knowing you are not alone can be healing in and of itself.

Don't be silent. You can do your bit against stigma by speaking out. Write about it. Blog about it. Tweet it. Speak at events. Share with friends. Your words might be the thing to instill courage in another person facing a similar challenge or change someone's mind as to the value of seeking mental health help.

Asking for Help Is a
Sign of Strength

Asking for help when we cannot help ourselves is a badge of strength, even though our culture often tries to convince us otherwise.

If any problem with the mind goes untreated, it does not go away by itself or get better by doing nothing. Asking for help is the necessary step to change yourself from being a victim into a survivor. It is the ultimate show of resilience in the face of adversity.

To go against the grain and defy generalizations and social stereotypes, like how "mental health problems make you weak," is a show of courage and strength because you are not just taking a stand against societal norms, but you are also confronting something scary.

I love the quote by author Haruki Murakami, "Pain is inevitable; suffering is optional." It so succinctly describes the fact that we will all experience pain, but we have absolute control in managing that pain and growing from whatever experience led us to it. We have a greater chance for early recovery if we identify these symptoms and ask for help.

The longer you live with any kind of mental health issue, the more dangerous it becomes. For instance, someone who is chronically depressed may stop eating properly, sleeping well, and going to doctor appointments. He or she becomes hopeless, and hopelessness can lead to destructive behavior, thoughts of self-harm, or suicide.

We are a country that self-medicates mental health issues with alcohol or drugs. We create a life-threatening downward spiral, as this negatively impacts our job performances and wrecks relationships and financial health. Living with mental health issues without getting help is giving up and simply existing in a black hole. Seeking help is, therefore, the smart and strong thing to do. It's impossible to be an expert in all areas of life, so it only makes sense to defer to professionals with expertise in an area that we know nothing about.

When we have a respiratory issue, we see a doctor. When we have cavities, we see the dentist. Any major home renovation or repair job goes to building contractors. Why should we treat mental health distress with any less action?

Recognize that you cannot treat depression on your own— the same way you can't solve your respiratory problem, fill your own cavity, or repair your home. Seeking therapy when it is needed is a smart, compassionate, and courageous decision. It requires someone to be self-aware and takes a lot of work and commitment. If these are not signs of strength, I don't know what are.

Self-Assessment

If you are reading this book, it means you are seeking and open to change in your life. Evaluating your specific needs can be difficult. Here are a few tips to help you determine if you should seek outside help.

You feel overwhelmed all the time. Life is not always easy. I don't have all the answers, and neither do you. However, there are times when you will feel like you no longer have any idea how to continue managing a life that seems to be spiraling out of control. Sometimes, you don't even know why you feel so stressed, but you know that something is overwhelming you. This could be your first sign.

You keep making self-defeating choices. You tell yourself that you won't ever do that thing again, and then you go right back and do it. If there are certain damaging behaviors that you know are not right, yet you keep on going back to them, you may need to see a therapist. This might be engaging in risky behaviors, such as having unprotected sex, overeating, drinking too much, engaging in extramarital affairs, and so forth.

You feel trapped. Sometimes you feel like you are in a loop. You take jobs that don't make you feel happy. You can't say no to your friends. You can't get out of a cycle of debt even if you are making good money. Sometimes, therapy can help you get to the very bottom of the not-so-clear reasons why you keep making choices that don't work.

You feel like nobody understands. Perhaps there are issues in your life and stuff you are dealing with that no one around you gets, no matter how much you try to explain.

You react disproportionately to events, and your emotions are out of whack. If you keep having huge emotional responses to little triggers, it could be that you have long-lasting suppressed emotions that you have not adequately dealt with or experiences that you haven't healed from.

You feel like your life is a lie. Perhaps you feel like the life you are living is not authentic and that you are merely pretending. You know in your heart of hearts that real happiness comes when you take the time to listen to yourself and quit trying to impress others, but you cannot stop. So you go through life feeling inauthentic, but you are unable to tell any close family or friends how you're feeling

You think nobody listens to you or truly hears you. You may be in a situation where you are struggling, and people don't seem to understand your struggle. For example, you just broke up with your partner, and you want to vent and rage, but your friends were also his friends, and they don't get your frustration. Or maybe you are struggling with your sexuality, and this is something your loved ones cannot handle.

You suffer from extremely low moods every now and then. Perhaps you have very good days, and then you have extremely bad days. The best thing you can do for yourself is to seek therapy during the times that you feel strong because it can become tougher and tougher to harness the energy to make that call when the blues hit.

You are fed up with acting strong all the time. Perhaps you feel like you have to keep acting strong even when you don't feel like you are. You don't want to act like you are vulnerable, and you don't want it to look like you need help. It's essential to realize that genuine help actually involves being courageous enough to allow yourself to be seen as less than perfect.

You suffer from anxiety or constantly have intrusive thoughts. It is a normal human thing to worry about stuff occasionally. It is, however, not normal to be so consumed by worry that it causes physical symptoms or eats up a significant part of your day.

Loss of interest and apathy. This manifests as becoming apathetic to the world around you or no longer bothering with the things that used to make you happy.

Hopelessness. If you constantly feel like there is no future for you and you have lost the motivation to do anything for yourself, it could be a sign that you are suffering from depression or another mental health condition.

Social withdrawal. There are those of us who feel better when we are able to spend time alone. In fact, introverts require space to recharge their batteries to function effectively. This is understandable. If you, however, are constantly distressed when you are around others or genuinely fear being around others, this is a different matter that might be hindering your life.

There are no hard and fast rules about when or why to see a therapist since there are many reasons for seeking therapy, some more obvious than others, but each as valid as the other. Every human being is unique, and we do not all suffer the same way. Therefore, there is no computing mental or emotional stress and distress.

The rule of thumb is if you are generally not feeling at peace with your life, therapy is something you should seriously consider.

How Do You Know You Need Help?

We often use the word *stress* to describe a variety of feelings we're experiencing when it's difficult to deal with feelings or situations. *Stress* isn't the best word to describe those moments where everything feels like it's weighing you down, slowing your pace, numbing your senses, pulling you in a million directions, yet not moving anywhere. I prefer the term *overwhelm* because it more accurately describes the overall general feeling of *weighted-down-ness*.

With so many people living with different levels and types of daily overwhelm, it looks and feels different for each person. Unlike the *fight or flight* response of stress, overwhelm is the *freeze* response. We live consumed by deadlines, traffic, financial worries, endless streams of information, family responsibilities, perfectionist tendencies, and so forth. This overwhelm grows layer upon layer, weighing on us. Overloaded with the weight, it can short-circuit our lives, leaving us stuck in the rut of overwhelm.

Short-term, situational overwhelm may be highly stressful, but living with the chronic weight each day can become unbearable. Whether a single catastrophic event or a buildup of smaller events forms an avalanche of *overwhelm*, it can sneak up behind us or hit us over the head.

What aspects of your life reflect the overall overwhelm of living full-on in today's complex society? How does overwhelm manifest in your daily life? What does overwhelm feel like for you?

Consider your typical day—work, meetings, school, children, intimate relationships, family, friends, exercise, meditation, hobbies, sex, food, chores, errands, cleaning, emails, social media, and so on. Do you neglect huge sections of this list to make time for other areas of life? Do you prioritize chores over self-care, or work above friendships? You're not alone.

At times, you may find yourself hit by overwhelm in many areas in your life over and over again, like a growing wave. It may start with working longer hours due to job expectations and financial pressures, then it impacts your relationships if people don't see you as much, and it eventually targets your health from a lack of exercise and poor eating from not taking care of yourself. A hamster wheel of overwhelm.

Recognizing the early signs of overwhelm alerts you to the start of a process before it consumes your whole life. Where are you at now? What do you struggle to truly appreciate and celebrate about your life? Which of the questions below are hard to answer, and which do you long to know the answers to?

1. What areas of your life are typically overwhelmed?
2. How are they overwhelmed: stuck, weighed down, and/or ignored?
3. What keeps them stuck?
4. What are your *gifts* (your fantastic talents)?
5. How are you using your *gifts*?
6. How are you undervaluing them?
7. What is your passion?
8. What does it feel like to live your life *on purpose*?

Take a moment and write down the things that make you feel overwhelmed. By sitting down and thinking about what overwhelms you and physically writing them down, you'll be able to identify areas you need to change. You may be surprised by the list you come up with when you actually spend time being mindful of the things causing you angst. It is by identifying these areas that you can begin to change them.

It's hard to enjoy life when buried beneath overwhelm, unable to budge or breathe. Overwhelm stifles your ability to listen clearly to your head and heart, or know and trust in yourself, your intuition, your inner wisdom. You live numb to yourself.

Ideally, when you see overwhelm more clearly on the horizon, you can enhance your awareness, consider options, make wise decisions, and take positive action. Hopefully, each time you build a stronger resiliency to future overwhelm and move into living your best life.

How to Find a Therapist Who Is Right for Your Needs

The most important thing in a therapist is how you connect with him or her. You need to feel connected to your therapist so you can be open and honest and trust that you will get the help you need. Here is what you should do to find the right therapist for you:

Start by collecting names from your health care provider. Insist on being given the entire provider list, not just one or two names from the list. Check with family and friends. You may be surprised that they have a good recommendation.

Check with professional bodies to find out about the therapist's expertise. It is important to find out if your intended therapist provides psychotherapy, can prescribe medications or not, if they have a specialty, and so forth.

Here are a few tips for finding the right therapist for you:

1. Ask around and keep an open mind when searching. Get recommendations from a doctor, a trusted friend, or family members.
2. Go to a licensed therapist for serious emotional or behavioral issues. The four types of licensed practitioners available to people seeking psychotherapy are psychiatrists, psychologists, clinical social workers, and licensed professional counselors. Seek an experienced, licensed mental health provider.
3. Find someone who does not try to fit the client to his or her preferred clinical approach. If a therapist realizes that his or her therapeutic approach isn't the right fit for you, they should tell you and recommend someone who might be a better fit for your specific needs.

4.   Look for someone who puts you at ease and has a sense of respon-sibility in creating a warm, conducive, and safe environment during therapy sessions. You and your therapist should also have chemistry or rapport. The treatment will never be successful unless you feel comfortable being open, honest, and vulnerable with your therapist.

5.   Pick a therapist who is supportive of your lifestyle and knowledge-able in dealing with your type of issues to help you find the kind of solutions you seek.

6.   Know what you want from therapy. You should know where to start and why you are seeking help. Consider where you are in your treatment process and what you need right now as a client.

7.   You should consider your therapist's location as well as his or her availability that matches with your schedule.

8.   Find a therapist that you can afford. The cost of therapy can some-times scare us away from getting the help we need. However, don't let it stop you altogether. It might just be the best investment you ever make.

Your First Appointment

Your first appointment with a new therapist should be to determine if this is the therapist for you. At the first appointment you should feel things out and determine if this is some-body you want to continue to work with. Here are tips to arm yourself with at your first appointment.

Ask questions:

- How many years of practice does the therapist have?
- Has he or she treated people with your specific challenges before?
- What results did they achieve?

- Do they like to have an end plan? How will I know when therapy is no longer needed?
- If they don't feel like they can help, will they recommend you to another therapist?
- Do they subscribe to a specific type of therapeutic specialty?
- What are the policies about payment, fees, cancelations, missed appointments, and insurance?

After a few sessions with a new therapist, you'll want to consider your comfort level with that person and whether you feel the sessions are moving in the right direction for your goals. Some questions to consider:

- Am I comfortable with this person?
- Do I feel that he or she is really hearing what I am saying?
- Have they asked me enough questions? This is very important, and your first session should be filled with questions from the therapist, as this is the time he or she has to know you and become aware of all the challenges you're bringing to the table.
- Have you been asked the foreseeable or expected outcome from this therapy?
- Did he or she ask you how you hope your life would be post therapy?
- Have you established a therapy goal?
- Are you feeling okay with the resources at the therapist's disposal? For example, can he or she include you in a therapy group if that's what you need?
- Does the therapist make sense to you, and was he or she helpful in those first few sessions?

One Size Does Not Fit All

Finding the right therapist can be difficult. Just like in school, there were teachers you liked and really connected with and teachers whose classes you dreaded going to. When searching for a therapist, it's important that you feel comfortable with him or her. If you don't, then you won't open up, and you won't get out of therapy what you should.

If you find a therapist and it doesn't feel right, then look for someone else. You don't owe them anything, and they won't take it personally if you need to see someone else. Therapy is for you, your time to be selfish. Don't worry about hurting anyone's feelings. Take care of you and only you when finding the right therapist.

I started therapy when I was six—family therapy mandated by the courts. My brother, being born with genetic issues compounded by the abusive household we grew up in, had many behavioral and emotional issues. I remember really liking my first therapist, an older man, very kind and soft-spoken. His office felt warm and welcoming. Whereas my own father was cold and angry all the time, here was a man who was kind and compassionate and listened to me.

Over the years, I've had several different types of therapists. There were a few I liked and connected with, and many I didn't. I tend to gravitate toward male therapists. This is probably because my first therapist was a male, and it was such a positive experience.

I once saw a therapist when I was suffering one of my worst bouts of depression. She put me on medication, but it was the wrong medication for me. I'm pro antidepressants, but the issue is there are so many on the market that it's hard to find the right one. I've tried at least five different ones over the years, and each one had at least one negative side effect. Some I could live with easier than others. This therapist put me on medication and at each visit insisted that I fill out a mental health form to gauge my level of depression and suicidal ideations. One time I went to her office completely distraught, and when all I wanted to do was talk, she insisted on having me fill out this same form I always filled out. I told her I didn't want to this time. She kept insisting without listening to me. I left and never went back.

I didn't leave because she wanted me to fill out the form. I understand why she wanted me to do it. I left because I needed her to listen to me and she wouldn't. She wouldn't do what needed to be done and was so stuck in forms and processes that she didn't give me what I needed. There was no compassion or understanding. I didn't feel secure or cared for by her. I knew it was time for me to find someone else, someone who would be a better fit for my needs. She may have been great for someone else, but she wasn't the right fit for me.

I was on the hunt again for someone who was right for me. At the time, money was tight, so I was looking for a therapist who would either operate on a sliding scale or one where the cost was covered by insurance. Cost can be an inhibiting factor in finding the right person as therapy can get very expensive. Sadly, the government isn't as helpful as it should be in terms of assisting people who need access to mental health resources. If they did, they would probably save a great deal in other areas.

After a lot of searching, I found an organization that offered free mental health services, and one of the doctors there was doing cognitive behavioral therapy (CBT). I had heard great things about CBT and was open to trying it. The thing about CBT is it's not talk therapy. Some therapists may do both talk therapy with CBT, but this person didn't. He was fine enough, however I didn't feel that I ever connected with him. Because it wasn't talk therapy, it didn't matter as much. I wasn't opening up old wounds and traumas where I had to be vulnerable.

Over the weeks I saw him, he gave me CBT exercises to do that were great. I learned a lot about myself and how I dealt with experiences and feeling. I enjoyed the process of CBT but finally realized that at that time in my life, I needed talk therapy more than CBT tools. So, I left that therapist and was once again in search of a new one.

I specifically wanted help getting over the feelings of rejection I had surrounding my birth family. I told my new therapist that I've suffered severe trauma in my life and felt like I had a good grasp on many of the emotions surrounding the various traumatic experiences I've had. However, this specific trauma was one experience that I'd never been able to get past. I wanted to put the work in to dealing with this *one* issue and this one issue alone.

A potential issue with jumping from therapist to therapist is having to drudge up all those old wounds. You have to tell and retell a story, which is difficult. I sat in this therapist's office over three appointments going through my childhood and the feelings I had about being adopted and then finding my birth parents and being rejected brutally and painfully. It was awful. I cried and was drained. But I was hopeful. After all his listening and questions, I expected him to help me start working on developing a coping strategy to deal with the negative feelings I had because of this trauma.

I was ready. I walked into his office on the fourth visit, full of hope. I'd done the hard part, now I was ready and willing to put in whatever work I had to put in to feel better. I sat down in his chair and waited. He looked at me and told me to build a house in my mind. In that house, I was to put this trauma and close the door and pretend it doesn't exist. What? I couldn't believe that I spent all that time sharing my story when all he suggested was for me to shut the door on it. I wanted his help. I needed his help. I told him this was the only issue I wanted to work on, and he told me to build a house and ignore this issue.

I was devastated, got up, and left the therapist's office never to return. It hurt and was emotionally exhausting.

Because I've had several different therapists, I'm able to know what I like and what I don't like. I tend to gravitate toward therapists who will talk to me, who will ask probing questions and get me to think about things in ways I wouldn't necessarily have come to on my own. I had another therapist for years who reminded me of that kind man I saw as a child. He was compassionate and caring and made me feel important and validated. Whenever I needed help or a boost, I would go see him because I knew he was always there whenever I needed him. Sadly, he retired, and I had to find someone else.

What I want you to know is that not all therapists are the same, and not all therapy is for everyone. It may take you time to find the right person, but when you do, it's worth it. I'm very grateful for the handful of therapists I had in my life who helped me immensely, and there were several. Don't give up if you find a therapist you don't connect with. Love yourself enough to keep going. Keep seeking the help you need. If you don't do it for yourself, who will?

Getting the Best Help for You

TIP 1: You don't have to go back

Please understand that you do not have to return for a second appointment if the therapist does not answer your questions, if you do not feel comfortable with them, or if the relationship is just not a good fit.

Here are some reasons you might want to keep searching for a therapist after your first session:

- The therapist tells you that you might be dealing with treatment issues that fall outside the scope of his or her expertise or competence, and they're not sure they can really help you as much as you need to be helped.
- The therapist may have a conflict of interest. For example, this might happen if he or she already has another client who you know well, and the therapist thinks that the dual clinical relationship may create messy boundaries.
- The therapist may respond to you very strongly in a way that would interfere with his or her ability to maintain objectivity or remain empathic to you and your issues. For example, a therapist with very strong personal ideologies about religious affiliation, sexual orientation, or lifestyle in general, might not be a good fit for you if you have opposing views from him or her.

TIP 2: Don't lie

This may seem obvious, but it's worth mentioning. It's easy to lie to a therapist or not share the whole truth. The reason you are going to therapy can be difficult to face, and opening up and being fully honest can be hard, especially if it's an issue you haven't spoken about before. If we've always kept things to ourselves, then it's hard to go into a session and be totally vulnerable.

When I went to therapy in my twenties, I lied to the therapist because I was too embarrassed to be totally honest, which defeated the purpose of being there. I'd leave feeling no better. A therapist can only help you if they know and understand what you truly need help with. The therapist won't judge you, and they've probably heard worse. It's your time and money, so use it wisely. Make a conscious effort to be open and honest and catch yourself if you are lying or holding back information that could help in your recovery.

TIP 3: If you are prescribed medication, take it

The reality is that some of us dealing with mental health issues will have to be placed on medication to alleviate our symptoms. It is important to realize that medications are not cures, they only treat symptoms, and those symptoms will probably return if you quit taking them.

Following a strict medication regime, whether you are dealing with mental health or physical ailments, can be tough. We are tempted to miss a dose or two or three or so many that we lose count, especially when our medication comes with unpleasant side effects.

But these medications were given for a reason—to help us feel better; to alleviate the symptoms and make life more manageable. It is important to never stop taking them, even if they are an inconvenience, without talking to your doctor first.

I've been on and off medications since I was sixteen. Sometimes my serotonin level gets so low that I need a boost to get out of the deep depression my brain has sucked me into. Going on medication doesn't have to be a lifetime commitment. Sometimes you only need it for a short time, and when you start feeling better, you can go off of it, slowly and with help.

The first time I was on antidepressants, I didn't understand withdrawal and having to ween yourself off this type of medication. I got the flu and kept throwing up my medication, so I stopped taking it. The flu became much worse and nearly impossible to bear. I ended up in the hospital because the symptoms were so bad. I was in the worst pain of my life. After much questioning, the doctor finally realized it was withdrawal I was suffering from because I stopped my medication cold turkey. As soon as I started retaking my medication, I started to feel much better.

Medication can help, and you should never feel bad about having to go on medication when suffering from depression. Make sure to follow the instructions carefully and always talk to your doctor if you're ready to stop. Never ever stop cold turkey.

TIP 4: Surround yourself with people who genuinely care

When it comes to mental health, and especially when you're recovering from a mental illness, I cannot stress enough how important it is to be surrounded by understanding, loving, and supportive people. It is essential that the people who are close to you, that you allow into your circle, be the people who can raise you up and encourage you to get better.

It is important that you surround yourself with people who will listen to you, who will not ignore you, who won't consider your issues as insignificant (even when they don't understand them), and who will not continue with any toxic behavior toward you when this is brought to light.

Yes, these people will not always understand what you're going through, but it is important that they allow you to open up to them as you journey toward recovery. While that friend or family member may be unable to give you the right advice on how to handle your problem, the support they offer should make you feel like you are not alone in the world.

TIP 5: Don't quit therapy if one therapist didn't feel right

If you didn't feel comfortable during your first therapy session, please don't get discouraged and give up. Like I mentioned earlier, not every therapist will be a perfect fit. You may have to interview a few in order to find the right one, just like you would shop around until you found the perfect dentist. You wouldn't commit yourself to a lifetime of dental pain, so don't commit yourself to a lifetime of emotional pain just because your first therapy session did not work out. I urge you not to quit looking. You will find a therapist that will work for you and your needs.

I encourage you not to delay one moment longer if mental health issues are creating barriers in your life. Just like with a physical ailment, the sooner you seek help, the easier it will be to heal.

Not seeking help means opening yourself up to the possibility of getting even worse. A mental or emotional disorder that is left untreated can disrupt your relationships, jeopardize job opportunities, harm performance at work and in life, and increase your risk for substance abuse and addiction.

By not seeking help, you are choosing to live in a black hole. Love yourself enough to find a way to climb out of that hole. Yes, it is daunting. Yes, it is scary. But it is also liberating. I urge you to take the first step to get out of the darkness you're living in. It is perhaps the most courageous thing you can do for yourself and your loved ones.

CHAPTER TWELVE

Share Your Life Lessons

You're not a victim for sharing your story.
You are a survivor setting the world
on fire with your truth. And you never know
who needs your light, your warmth,
and raging courage.

—Alex Elle

There are two types of people in the world, over-sharers and everyone else. The term over-sharer has a negative connotation to it, and I wish it didn't. People who choose to open up and share are often classified as over-sharers because people aren't used to others being so open and vulnerable. It's not easy putting yourself in a position of vulnerability. But if you did, you would not believe the positive impact you could have on yourself and others.

I am an over-sharer now, but I wasn't always. I used to be ashamed of my life, and I never wanted anyone to know how bad it was. I never knew anyone like me, so I was embarrassed to talk about my experiences.

From the outside, our family looked normal. We had a house, two parents, two children—a boy and a girl. A millionaire's family, as society tends to call it. Little did people know the hell that was going on behind closed doors.

It wasn't until I started therapy that I realized my horrors were not unusual. So many other families suffered from similar issues, and other children faced traumas too. I wasn't alone. Forced group therapy showed me this. At first, I was against group therapy. I didn't want to talk about my problems with total strangers and risk being judged. I didn't want people to think there was something wrong with me.

The first time I went to group therapy, I went with the intention of not saying a word. I sat and listened to two children my age talk about their families and the issues they were living through. This was my "eureka" moment. I wasn't alone, and they weren't alone. I started feeling *normal*, and I use the word normal loosely because what happened to me was not normal and should never be viewed as such. What I mean by normal is that it wasn't happening *just* to me. Horrible things weren't happening because I was a bad person who deserved it. These bad things were happening to other people, which meant I wasn't the cause of these traumatic experiences.

Be a sharer. You don't have to be an over-sharer, but verbalizing your experiences, especially ones you've learned from, can be very powerful. Share your life lessons, not just your struggles. This allows you to give back to people and possibly offer them solutions to their issues.

Don't Bottle It Up;
Sharing Is Good for the Soul

Life is many things: an adventure, a story, a journey, or an enduring series of experiences. It is full of moments that transform into memories, some of which are great and some painful. Whether good or bad, those moments shaped who we are today, and the great thing about them is that they are shareable.

I used to be embarrassed about the things I went through in life. The traumas I experienced were horrific and embarrassing. I hated my life. I hated my past. Then, through a lot of personal inner work, I realized that all of those experiences I had, both bad and good, made me who I am today. The compassion and understanding I have, the strength and resiliency, are all because of getting beyond the experiences I've had in my past.

Too many times, we dwell on bad things and wish them away. I wished many of my experiences didn't happen to me, but I can't change the past. I can only change the way I view it and how I let those negative experiences affect my present and future. I am who I am today because of what I lived through. I choose to love myself. I choose to be a survivor and not a victim. And now, I choose to share my stories with others because if I can help just one person, then the sharing is worth it.

As humans, we are wired to draw lessons from the stories of others. We see this when professors share stories of their industries so that their students can learn from their real-world experiences. A parent will share with her teenage daughter the costly mistakes she made as a teenager so that the daughter doesn't make the same mistakes. As humans, we are hardwired to learn through story.

It is essential to understand that others can learn from our traumatic experiences and the lessons we've learned as a result of those experiences. It can be healing to share these with others.

One of the best things I did to cope with being rejected by my birth parents was to share my story on YouTube. It was the most cathartic thing I've ever done because of the response of strangers sharing their stories with me. It gave me a different perspective on a situation that I thought I understood. One birth mother commented about her experience giving her child up for adoption:

So much happens as the decades pass. Unimaginable feelings of grief and loss, of wandering aimlessly in life until you eventually accept your child is gone for good; a process that takes so many years. To finally reach that place and tuck it away until it becomes a rare memory, and to build a new life, an entire life, and then to suddenly be brought right back to those moments and memories in time is what happens when the adult child comes looking. It takes a high level of courage to accept the feelings and all of the explaining to family, friends, acquaintances, coworkers, and everyone who knew you before. Your identity is gone; your secrets are revealed. It is overwhelming, and perhaps that is why some parents don't or won't engage with their biological child. Oh, the courage I had to find deep down in my heart to accept any embarrassment I would feel over my past and yet try to explain that I was not ashamed of my son. I was proud of him. I missed him. I loved him. I love him still. Yes, I will take any fallout that may come because to love is to risk. Your biological parents may not have heroic love just yet, but don't give up on them in your heart. One day they may discover it.

It was this perspective and insight from a total stranger that helped in my healing. It was the first time I understood that my birth parents' rejection wasn't because of me personally. It could be because of several other reasons that I won't ever understand. It was at that point that I began to do the work on letting go of the pain. If I had never shared my story publicly, I would not have received such profound insight from a birth mother.

Benefits of Sharing

Keeping our emotions bottled up can cause problems down the line, launching negative attacks on our emotional, mental, and even physical health. When we ruminate on problems in our own heads for too long, we magnify these problems and make them worse than they actually are. Sharing our experiences with others, on the other hand, allows us to be free from the pain of those experiences, enabling us instead to draw the lessons from them.

Some experiences rob us of our ability to speak up, especially when we internalize them for too long. For example, a battered spouse who doesn't speak to someone about the abuse eventually starts to believe that there is something in his or her nature that attracts abuse. Not dealing with this mentality before moving on to another relationship increases the chances for the next relationship to also be an abusive one.

However, when we share our experiences, we feel empowered through finding our voices. We can then be ambassadors of our life circumstances rather than victims. We can show the world what we are made of and prove to ourselves that our lives are worth fighting for.

If self-empowerment comes when you find your voice,

imagine what you can do for others. You can bring hope, which is something we all need. We all look for a light at the end of that dark road. Your hindsight can become another person's foresight. You help others when you share your stories of struggle and the lessons learned. Others will realize that they are not alone, that someone like you has been in a similar predicament, and it is possible to make it out alive. This might be all they need to get through a desperate time.

You might not know it, but your body and your brain get a lot of benefits from simply talking. Recent research from UCLA shows that *affect labeling*, a fancy term for expressing your feeling in words, has a way of diminishing your emotional response. As you keep expressing yourself, your brain and body become less stressed over that issue. For example, getting into a car not long after having been in a car accident can be emotionally overwhelming. Talking through the experience, however, will eventually lessen the emotional reaction.

Research from Southern Methodist University suggests that undergoing talk therapy or writing about traumatic experiences can have a positive impact on your health and immune system, stating that holding back thoughts and suppressing emotions can be bad for your physical health. Because you are working hard to contain your negative feelings, you put an excessive amount of pressure on your body and brain and are more susceptible to falling ill or just feeling plain awful.

While sharing your experience or entering into therapy is not a fix-all solution, it does work, just like eating well and exercising will contribute to overall well-being. In the same way, talking about what you are feeling will contribute to your emotional well-being.

It is an uncomfortable feeling to admit our moments of weakness, struggles, or failures to others. However, publicly owning our moments of vulnerability can be surprisingly gratifying and the greatest badge of courage anyone can wear.

If you struggle with feelings of worthlessness and weakness, sharing your experience with others allows you to practice courage and gives you an inner strength that you didn't know you had before. When I shared my story of my birth parents' rejection on YouTube, I was so nervous to post such a deeply personal story online for everyone to judge. However, I put my fears aside to share my story in the hopes that I could make just one person feel less alone in their hurt, and I was beyond amazed at the response.

Complete strangers opened up and shared their rejection stories with one another in the comments and the level of support they gave one another was incredible. People emailed me to say how grateful they were that I shared my story and that it made them feel less alone. Putting myself out there gave me a strength and confidence that I never imagined I could have. It was the best form of therapy I'd ever had.

There is nothing as comforting as being able to open up and share your struggles with someone who has been there and understands when others don't. There is also a priceless value from taking advice from an individual who's been through your experience and has come out on the other end.

For example, people who've never suffered depression don't have the tools to give you proper advice, no matter how well intentioned they might be. Someone who's suffered through depression and is doing better will be able to listen to you, understand you, and perhaps share one or two strategies for coping effectively. This person helps you to see that there is hope. Sharing our experiences creates a community of support.

Sharing your problems with others gives them insight into you and your actions. Sometimes, if people think you are doing okay, they will treat you a certain way or react a certain way without understanding that your behavior is a result of whatever trauma or negative experiences you are going through.

You may have a lot of genuinely compassionate people in your life, but if they don't know what you have experienced or are experiencing, they don't know what area of your life they need to apply that compassion to.

For example, if you are the primary caregiver for your ailing wife and still have to go to work, your colleagues might not understand why you are stressed most of the time and never in the mood for an occasional quick drink after work. Sharing your circumstances allows friends and colleagues to extend kindness and compassion to you.

When you open up to others, you often gain new perspectives and may discover solutions that you'd been unable to reach on your own. For example, while battling infertility can be terribly isolating, there are actually other people around you going through the same agony in silence. Opening up to one another can help you find solutions, perhaps in the form of a hormonal treatment you could take, or in the way of visiting a fertility clinic that deals with your exact problem.

When you share your story with another person, especially the stories that you still are not too clear about yourself, you get the chance to gather your thoughts and feelings properly so that you have clarity on the matter at hand, perhaps for the first time. Even if the other person does not understand and questions your actions, the fact that you spoke about it, or even had to defend your actions, can in and of itself be cathartic.

When I shared my rejection video, a few people criticized me by saying I was wrong to reach out to my birth family. I didn't realize my inner demon had been telling me the same thing. I didn't even realize I felt this way until I defended my actions to the trolls who left those comments. I was addressing something that I didn't even consciously realize was bothering me, and I felt so much lighter and stronger in the actions I had taken.

I am incredibly passionate about destigmatizing mental health issues, and I find that brave individuals who share their experiences offer us all an extremely effective way to begin meaningful conversations about mental health. The reality is that the more we have conversations about mental health, the more we educate others and the less the stigma has room to thrive.

I am encouraged today by the way that business leaders, athletes, celebrities, and even royalty are opening up about mental health issues, but we can do more. There is no underestimating the power of sharing one's experiences to normalize what is a deeply personal and often sensitive issue for many. This will help to reduce the stigma surrounding mental health and encourage people who need help to reach out for it.

Obstacles to Sharing Our Experiences

There are many reasons we may loathe opening up about our experiences. For some of us, it has everything to do with the way we were raised. If you were brought up in an atmosphere where showing vulnerability was seen as weakness, opening up to others can seem nearly impossible.

Emotional language is a learned skill, and if we are not taught this from our early years, we'll have problems verbalizing vulnerability as adults. If you have opened up as an adult and been flat out rejected, this may make you wary to be vulnerable again. In other cases, we worry that vocalizing our fears will make them real.

Not having the emotional skill of vulnerability brings with it a sense of isolation and loneliness. Learning to work through hindrance will help you to discover that you are not, and never will be, alone.

How to Share Your Experience and Open Up to People

Be yourself. We are often tempted to put on a front so that others will connect better with us. We fear others will judge our true selves. However, this is not a sustainable way of life— pretending and wearing a façade. You don't know who will like the real you until you let yourself shine.

It should be a daily goal to be your most authentic self. Never change your personality or do things you normally wouldn't do to earn someone else's interest or friendship.

Ask questions. Good listeners have a good chance of being

listened to as well. If you can get others to loosen up in conversations and allow them to tell you about themselves, you will learn how to speak more openly. Ask questions. Show interest in the answers they give. Get to know people genuinely. When you do, you will have less difficulty opening yourself up to them when your burdens become too heavy.

Be candid. When we approach touchy subjects, we tend to sugarcoat the conversation or make an effort to make the issue sound pleasant. Be sensitive to other people's feelings, but always say it how it is. When you do, you'll be regarded as honest and forthright, and people are more likely to listen and truly hear what you are saying.

Let them know what you're looking for. If you are looking for advice, say so. If you are just looking for a listening ear, let them know. When I was going through infertility issues, all I wanted people to say was, "That sucks, it must be so hard!" I didn't want people to solve my problem. I didn't want to hear, "Just stop trying." Or "It'll happen when you least expect it." Or "If it's meant to be, it will be." These sentiments didn't help. All I wanted was someone to tell me what I was going through sucked. Someone who showed me empathy and understanding. Not someone who tried to solve the problem.

If you don't ask for what you need, then you'll end up getting something you don't want, and you might resent the person and close yourself off.

Know what you want to say. It's easy to shy away from speaking up because all the words get so jumbled in our heads, and we don't quite know how to say what we want to say. The right words in your head might never make it out of your mouth. This gives the person you're talking to the opportunity to jump in with their own words, further confusing your thoughts.

Yes, it is healthy to talk about our feelings, but it is also great to take the time to properly digest and gather our thoughts before we speak. This is why I find journaling helpful. It is a great way to commit your feelings to paper first, especially when you are the type that struggles with conversations.

Talk to the right people. Not everyone you know will be receptive to your struggles. You may have some fun friends who you love spending time with, but perhaps you can't be vulnerable with them because they never take anything seriously. These are not the people to share your precious and perhaps painful experiences with. It is important to protect yourself by creating a safe space for your story sharing. A friend or family member who is patient, who listens, and who you have found to be empathetic in previous matters might be the one to open up to first.

You will have a better connection with some people more than you have with others, and these people will be easier for you to share your feelings with. When you have a difficult subject to discuss, it's often easier to do it with people you feel closer to, or who you feel will understand.

Talk to a therapist. There are times when unrealistic thought patterns and negative thoughts are so crippling that you cannot talk to just anyone about it, even when you know you should. This is where talk therapy should come in. Therapy arms us with tools for social interactions and allows communication to become positive experiences rather than agonizing nightmares.

Try group therapy. Seeking therapy within a group offers

support and guidance, helping people to share their personal feelings and experiences with people who understand just what they are talking about. These people have been in the same place that you've been, and their support can help relieve stress, guilt, or pain.

For example, a veteran suffering from PTSD may be hard-pressed to find family members or friends who understand the anxiety and depression he feels. Other veterans will, however, get him, and sometimes the only place to connect with another veteran is in a group setting.

The principal advantages of group therapy include being able to receive the support and encouragement of others, feeling less alone, getting to know role models who have successfully coped with a similar problem, and being a role model for others.

Stay in touch with friends and family. We live in a hectic world, and it is very easy to let our lines of communication with loved ones fall to pieces. When you don't communicate with your loved ones on everyday topics, it can be harder to do when you have a challenge that needs to be addressed. So do your best and make some effort to socialize as a part of your everyday life.

Have a sound support system in place. If you choose to share your story, especially publicly, it is vital that you have a great support system in place. The truth of the matter is that not everyone will react to your shared story the way you hope, and you may receive some unwarranted backlash and criticism for sharing your truth. There are idiots in the world who don't possess compassion, unfortunately.

It is, therefore, crucial that there is at least one person who will support you no matter what, someone who will comfort you and be there for you when negative responses attempt to break you. Be prepared for this if you desire to share your story with the broader public.

Opening Up to Others— Paying It Forward

Understanding the benefit of being heard when you speak up and being able to enjoy the emotional healing that it brings should make you want to pay it forward, and by this, I mean to be a listening ear for others when they want to share their own experiences.

If you have a friend or a family member or a colleague who is struggling with issues, it can be incredibly difficult to watch because you know too well the alienated feeling that comes with that.

You cannot force them to talk when they are not ready, as this may do more harm than good, but you can put yourself in a position that makes it is easy for them to approach you with their struggles. Here's how:

Choose the right time. When they are getting ready for work is perhaps not the best time to approach someone for a heart-to-heart talk. Try some time when you are both relaxed, and there are no distractions. If you try to delve into matters and they are just not ready, be patient and wait for another day. Opening a dialogue at least lets them know you are there to listen.

Listen and validate their feelings. It is not what is being said that matters, but the fact that we are talking and the other person is listening. If someone opens up to you, it's important that they feel heard, and you can do this by listening actively. Don't be distracted. Maintain good eye contact. Be open in your body language. Be sensitive. Don't invalidate the way that they feel, even if you don't quite understand it.

Share your own feelings. Sharing your own vulnerability might encourage them to do the same. When we are feeling bad, sometimes we just need to feel understood, even when the other person can't quite get it. Be this anchor of empathy for the other person. Show them that it's okay to express their feelings and that you are there to support them no matter what.

Steps to Stamp Out the Worry of What People Think of You

Every day can become a struggle for those of us who worry about what others think about them to such an extent, we begin to stay clear of what we view as difficult situations. We end up suffering from anxious thoughts, feelings, and actions. There are many reasons why we react to daily events in the way we do. The fundamental reason is what we have learned from past experiences and how our subconscious has interpreted events and turned associated feelings into a false belief.

The worry we feel when we think about how others view us can literally take control of our lives to the point where we avoid sharing any part of ourselves. However, there are things we can do that can help to take that control back and lead a life that feels confident and authentic. Knowing what you want out of sharing your life lessons will give you direct focus to your goal and a path of how to get there. Having this goal means that you can clearly remind yourself what it is you want so the worry of what others think is restricted.

It's not in human nature to be good at everything. Once we understand this and remember it daily, we can stop criticizing and hiding our weaknesses, accept them, and concentrate on improving the things that will benefit ourselves or the things that are working for us already.

Please understand what is right for one person might not be right for another. In life, there is not one option for all of us; if there were, we would all be leading the same, monotonous life. Whatever path we take in life, we will make good and bad decisions. It is almost inevitable that we'll beat ourselves up over the bad decisions we make. Instead, we should accept that everyone makes mistakes. The one way we can learn from our mistakes is to talk about them. Learn from them in order to move forward and make necessary changes.

If we decide to share our experiences with others, at some point, we will receive criticism. Criticism is unavoidable, and it can either be destructive or constructive. Constructive criticism allows you to build upon something you may not have mastered and reach your full potential. Destructive criticism exists as a negative comment that is said without compassion and maybe even malicious intent. This type of criticism is not beneficial at all, and we need to brush it off. This is easier said than done, but by practicing not caring what others think of you, you will become more resilient in time.

No matter how much you try, you can't control how others think or behave. You can only control what you do and say and how you act and treat others. Worrying too much about what other people think will cause you to change the way you think or act in order to change their thoughts or behaviors. This creates an air of inauthenticity in you that you don't want.

Remain genuine and authentic to who you are. Don't let others influence your behaviors, thoughts, and actions. You can't control what other people think, so let that go and only be concerned about what is right for you.

What Changes Do You Want?

Write down a list of things that you'd like to change in your life. Don't think too hard about the importance of those changes or how hard they would be to implement. Simply write a list without thinking of whether it would be possible to make those changes.

1. Now take that long list of changes you wrote down and put them in order of importance. What is the most important change you'd like to see in your life? It doesn't matter how difficult that change would be to make.

2. Go back to your original list and rewrite the list in order of ease. What changes would be the easiest to tackle?

3. Now you have two lists. List A is *important*; list B is *easy*. These lists have the same items but may have a different order.

What I want you to do is take the important list and select number one on that list. Write that down on a separate piece of paper. You are going to formulate a plan of how you can make that change happen.

- Write the change you want to see happen.
- What steps do you need to take to make that change?

- What obstacles might get in your way when you are trying to make that change?
- What are you going to do to overcome those obstacles?
- Write down a timeline for this to happen.

Keep this sheet in a place that you can reference often. Take the first step to making that change. Check off each step you take. Once you complete that change move on to the second most important thing on your list and repeat this exercise.

Do the same exercise with the easy list. You should have two changes on the go at any given time. The *easy* list may have items that aren't as important for you but are easy to complete. These are important because they will give you a sense of accomplishment and satisfaction. Your *important* list may take longer and be harder to accomplish. If you just focus on that list, it may make it harder for you to see your progress.

All changes in life require you to take action. You cannot get from point A to point B without putting one foot in front of the other repeatedly. Change is hard, relationships are hard, life is hard, but hard is okay. If challenges weren't difficult our successes wouldn't taste so sweet. Don't wait for change to happen in your life. Be the change you want to see in your life. If, occasionally, you are unsuccessful in completing the steps you imagined, simply revisit the list and write new steps to reach your goal—the change you want in your life. Life is not stagnant; it's always moving so remember to move and adapt with it.

Own Your Story

I love this quote by Brené Brown, a professor who has studied empathy, shame, vulnerability, and courage for the past twenty years: "When we deny the story, it defines us. When we own the story, we can write a brave new ending."

We are a sum total of all our experiences, so we are, in essence, our stories. Denying your story, and all the joys and pains that come with it, is killing off a little of yourself, day after day after day.

When you hide the truth of your life and the experiences that brought you here, you deny your story.

When you swallow back the pain and put on a brave face while falling to pieces inside, you deny your story.

When you deny your struggle with mental health and sugarcoat your story so that you are accepted as *normal* (whatever that means), you deny your story.

You are who you are today because of the experiences you stacked, one upon another, to get here. There is no denying that fact, and it is time to start owning your story.

Share it.

The more you keep your story to yourself, the harder you'll find it to be open and honest, and your alternative story will somehow become your truth. It is crucial that we accept ourselves, scars and all, and eventually learn to love those scars as part of who we are. They make us stronger, more authentic versions of ourselves.

Own your story by sharing it.

Own your pain until it no longer has a strangling hold on you.

Write your own brave ending. How wonderful would it be to own your experience, to admit it has been incredibly hard and that you've felt alone, but you now understand that you can have a fulfilling life because you've lived through and learned from your negative experiences?

This is the way to turn your traumatic experiences on their head and to write your own ending. I challenge you to do just this.

Don't become someone who's not living your truth.

Don't become someone who's not thriving in life.

Find the bravery to write your own story and share it with the world.

Bad things happen in life
but they do not define who you are
or the greatness you are capable of achieving.
Each new day offers up a chance for
you to not just survive—
but thrive in life.

—Laura Berg

ABOUT THE AUTHOR

LAURA BERG is a professor, author, entrepreneur, trained therapist, and award-winning parenting expert. Her YouTube channel *@LauraBergLife* is a top-ranked family channel with over 100 million views. Her first book, *The Baby Signing Bible*, has been a global success. She is the president and founder of an international American Sign Language institution called My Smart Hands Inc. that has over 200 instructors across North America. Among her many accolades, she has been named one of the Top 10 Mom Entrepreneurs by Yahoo Life, has won the SavvyMom Mom Entrepreneur of the Year Award, was awarded YouTube's Silver Play Button, and has appeared on Hallmark Channel's talk show *Home and Family*. As a trained therapist with a diploma in psychotherapy, Laura has two specialty certifications in cognitive behavioral therapy (CBT) and dialectical behavior therapy (DBT). Laura is currently a professor in the Professional Writing and Communications program at Humber College in Toronto and in the Advertising, Digital Media Management program at Durham College in Oshawa. She has also been a speaker at many social media, blogging, and entrepreneur conferences across North America including BlissDom, She's Connected, and #140Conf in NYC, where she was on the same bill as Deepak Chopra. In her spare time, Laura loves to travel and has been to over twenty countries.